HUMAN FERTILITY IN INDIA

Social Components and Policy Perspectives

HUMAN FERTILITY IN INDIA

*Social Components and
Policy Perspectives*

DAVID G. MANDELBAUM

UNIVERSITY OF CALIFORNIA PRESS
BERKELEY · LOS ANGELES · LONDON

University of California Press
Berkeley and Los Angeles, California
University of California Press, Ltd.
London, England
Copyright © 1974 by
David G. Mandelbaum
ISBN: 0-520-02551-2
Library of Congress Catalog Card Number: 73-84384
Printed in the United States of America

CONTENTS

PREFACE

THE spectacular successes during the twentieth century in lowering mortality rates and in prolonging human life around the world have guaranteed mankind a continuing problem of too many births. This is not a serious difficulty everywhere, but it is a great handicap in some of the poorest and largest of nations. A good many governments have been trying in recent decades to do something about the heavy burdens caused by parents who are now too prolific. Although firm comparative assessments of the various national programs cannot yet be made, the record so far shows that certain of the smaller of the developing countries are meeting the figures for decreased fertility they have set for themselves but that programs in the more populous developing nations have not yet succeeded in reducing fertility rates at the pace their respective plans proposed (Nortman 1972; Lapham and Mauldin 1972).

Proposals about how best to limit fertility rates have been characterized by three motifs. One gives prime place to political decisions. That is, if the political authorities would firmly establish a family planning agency and support it enthusiastically, birth rates will tumble. Such decisions, it turns out, are necessary to set a family planning movement going but are by no means enough to lower fertility rates effectively. The Government of India has established a large program and since 1965 has supported it strongly. Even in meetings of a village council, as one research worker learned in a village of Uttar Pradesh, family planning matters are regularly brought up, or so the record of the meeting ought to show, lest higher officials make trouble when they examine the records. The educational program has made such im-

pact that, as one experienced Indian demographer relates from
her own observations, "When an educated woman comes into a
village, the village women now expect that she has come to urge
them about family planning." Despite the massive official effort,
however, and its undoubted success in some aspects, the Indian
government's assessment is that their program has still far to go.

Another motif, and frequently a dominating one in program
planning, gives main weight to technology. Proponents of this
emphasis argue that the critical factor is the delivery of contraceptive devices and chemicals to eligible couples. Once that is
done efficiently, they believe, and provided that technological re-
finements continue to be made, then the flow of babies will surely
be stemmed and fertility rates will gravitate down to an acceptable level. A short answer to the technological enthusiasts has
been given by Burton Benedict. "Whether or not people use birth
control depends not on the availability of contraceptives but on
the availability of incentives to have fewer children" (1973:1046).

A third emphasis is on economic change. It is the argument
that when people raise their economic level, as the historical record shows, they tend to lower their birth rates. Therefore governmental efforts should be concentrated much more toward economic growth than toward fertility decline. This view prevailed
among Indian leaders for a number of years until the realization
grew that economic development was being severely handicapped
by the great concurrent increase in population. They saw that unless they restrained the population increase, they could not adequately raise the country's standard of living. They became convinced that economic development and fertility control are
closely related, so that progress in one reinforces advances in the
other. The emphasis in our present discussion is on the vital influence of social and cultural factors on fertility, and especially on
people's motivations to control their fertility.

The case of India is particularly cogent for program planning
in other countries, not only because it is one of the earliest and
largest of such programs but also because there are much more
data and analyses available for the Indian case than there are for
any other of the developing nations. This book begins with a

brief survey of the Indian family planning program. It then considers the reasons why most people in India want to have many children and under what circumstances they have traditionally limited their fertility. The relation to fertility of some major social and cultural differences is next considered, and also the traditional methods of birth control that have been used in India. Finally, suggestions are proposed for applying our knowledge of the social and cultural components of fertility behavior to family planning programs, both in the immediate future and in the longer time perspective.

The focus here is on fertility rather than on the larger subject of population. Such significant demographic matters as migration, demographic variations by states, and general mortality rates are not elaborated. The available data on some of the subjects considered are less than satisfactory. I have indicated some problems on which further research is particularly needed but have not tried to give here detailed evaluations of the research projects from which data are cited.

The research for this book was supported by grants from the Research Committee and the Center for South and Southeast Asian Studies, both of the University of California, Berkeley. I thank Betsey Cobb for her fine competence as research assistant, bibliographer, and typist. I am grateful for comments on the manuscript made by Ketayun Gould, Doranne Jacobson, Moni Nag, and Steven Polgar. Mrs. Amarjit Singh Bal helped in interviews with Indian men and women living in the Berkeley-Oakland area on the subjects of age at marriage and education. Anne Brower made preliminary editorial suggestions with her usual skill and good judgment. Grace Buzaljko ably completed the editorial work.

ONE

TOO MANY BABIES:
THE NATION'S CONCERN

WHEN a woman bears a child, when a man becomes a father, together they begin anew and continue again the strongest, most intimate social bonds of their lives. These bonds and all their acts in producing the child are moulded by their culture, by the expectations and standards commonly shared in their society. So to understand the fertility of any people, we must know something about their culture and society. To try to affect their fertility without guidance of that knowledge is to blunder about blindly.

A good many people in India practiced fertility control long before they had knowledge of modern contraceptive techniques. They did so for traditional social reasons and by methods traditional in the culture. These means and motivations are still current and, if properly understood, could be more effectively utilized in family planning efforts than they have been.

When I first wrote to that effect in 1949, I noted that a comprehensive analysis of these factors in Indian family life "must wait for further anthropological and sociological research" (1949:287). Although a good deal of such research has since been done, not much of it has been focused on the social and cultural aspects of fertility. Still, enough has been learned so that a review of the relevant findings may be useful.

Some of the basic demographic and historical facts about Indian population are given here for the general reader, though they are well known to most demographers and India specialists. The Indian Family Planning Programme was the first major governmental effort for fertility control, and it remains the largest national program in budget, personnel, and people covered. As such, it offers an important case example for other developing countries.

It also has special interest for those students of civilization who perceive in the modern population explosions and in governmental attempts to contain them a potentially important juncture in cultural evolution.

Population and the Nation's Prospects

The principal circumstances of Indian population growth can be quickly outlined. They are not basically different from what they were when I sketched them in 1949 and as others had noted them earlier, except that the numbers are larger, the adverse consequences even broader, the need for effective planning more apparent.

There were 547,949,809 people in India on Census Day, April 1, 1971, according to the Census count. This total is about 15.3% of the world's population. The increase from 1951 to 1961 was 108.8 million, at a rate for the decade of 24.7%. In that decade the people of India added to their number the equivalent of the population of Japan (the seventh most populous nation in the world) with some four million to spare.

The population situation as of 1971 was summarized by a leading Indian demographer, Dr. S. N. Agarwala. He noted that more than one million lives are added to India's numbers every month, and so the very considerable increases in agricultural and industrial production since Independence have not benefited the average Indian in similar proportion. Deficiencies in housing and education are great. Agarwala and other observers have pointed out that the steadily increasing number of mouths to feed and youngsters to support puts heavy strains on every aspect of the nation's economy and well-being. Broad improvements in agricultural production become more difficult, unemployment rises, political turbulence is quickened (see Agarwala 1971:8; Dasgupta 1970; Kamat 1971). The sheer increase in numbers increasingly hampers the nation's vigorous efforts to alleviate poverty and raise the standard of living.

The extent of that poverty has been indicated in a study prepared by members of the Indian School of Political Economy, Poona (Dandekar and Rath 1971). The authors take as the criterion of poverty an income that is not enough to give a person an average diet of 2250 calories a day, an intake considered to be minimally adequate under Indian conditions. (The average intake in the U.S. is about 3110 calories.) They conclude that in 1968–69 about 40% of the rural population and 50% of the urban were below that level (*ibid.*:143).[1] One study of available food in India between 1959 and 1968 shows that among the eight major categories of foodstuffs, there was an increase only in wheat and fish. The author asks, "What is the cause of the deteriorating food position during these 10 years of planned development?" And he gives the unequivocal answer, "The factor responsible for the situation is the steady rise in population" (Shetty 1971).

A large population and a 2.47% average annual rate of increase for the decade (2.2% geometric increase) are not of themselves fatal to economic development. Indeed, strong economic advances have been made in particular regions of India and in certain sectors of the economy. But the whole development effort tends to be shackled by the pervasive constraint resulting from population growth. Thus one study of human resources in India tells of the grave problems of the "manpower explosion of the '70s." The babies born in the population surge of 1955–65 will turn fifteen during that period, most will be ready to try to earn their living then, and the economy will not provide employment for many. No program of family planning, this study states, can have the slightest effect on these difficult problems. The economically surplus people have already been born and are growing into adulthood (Population Bulletin 1970:8).

The President of India, V. V. Giri, put the matter succinctly in a public statement of August 1970. "At the current rate of increase, our population will double in the next 28 years, reaching the incredible figure of one billion before the turn of the century.

1. Of several published appraisals of the study, one critic wrote that an average intake of 2250 calories does not necessarily mean a nutritionally balanced diet and that Indian diets tend to be deficient in protein (Medhora 1971:545). Another writer stated that by his calculation only some 11% of the urban population was undernourished, but he agreed that at least 33% of the rural population could not afford enough calories for an adequate diet (Madalgi 1971).

With the birth-rate remaining high and the mortality rate being reduced sharply, unless we devise concrete methods of checking the rate of population growth, it is difficult for us to assure even a minimum economic wherewithal to our population." This great problem, it should be noted, is an outcome of resounding successes in reducing mortality. To cope with it, a governmental program was begun in 1951, four years after Independence. The alternative was to leave the matter to individual and nongovernmental initiatives, hoping that Indian couples would eventually produce fewer children because of the same persuasions that convinced men and women in industrialized countries to do so. Prime Minister Indira Gandhi explained the reasons for rejecting that alternative, "Our own country, so marked by mass poverty, cannot leave it to individual motivation—because such motivation comes only after a certain level of literacy or economic betterment has already been reached. . . . It is because we cannot afford to wait until such consciousness becomes widespread, that we in India require well-planned official programmes, which are implemented with determination" (1969:5).

The Family Planning Programme: First Steps

Once a governmental program for family planning (as it was soon called) was initiated, an imperative first step was to let the people of India know the simple fact, then known to relatively few of them, that modern contraceptive methods exist and that it is desirable to use them. The task of communicating to hundreds of millions of villagers and townspeople that there are such things as intrauterine devices (IUDs), sterilization operations, and other contraceptive methods has been a large undertaking; persuading people to use these methods is a far knottier task.

Convincing India's political leaders to give high priority to family planning took some time, even though Indian social activists had sounded alarms for decades (see Pathare 1966:44–47; Bose 1970b:29–34). One of the first high officials to give such warning was A. Gopalaswami in his report, as Registrar-General, of the 1951 Census of India. He called attention to the desperate race between food and population and concluded that there would not be enough food for India's people until they could reduce their rate of increase. At that time, as Gopalaswami later noted, Prime Minister Nehru felt that he was unduly pessimistic and believed that the nation's chief problem was that of underdevelopment rather than of overpopulation (Sovani 1952:67–68; Nehru 1965:406–407; Weiner 1970:15). It was not that Nehru was opposed to fertility limitation, but that he and other policy makers saw the population issue as a diversion from the more fundamental challenge of economic development. They held that expanded production was the fundamental issue in raising the level of living; family planning could only remove a constraint. The grievous weight of that constraint was not yet appreciated, nor were the political leaders sure about how people would perceive governmental efforts to induce them to have fewer children.

Nevertheless, a budgetary provision for family planning was included in the First Five-Year Plan for the years 1951–56, and the Indian government became one of the first in the world to include family planning in its national policy. But the funds allocated for it were meager and the program was very modest. Some clinics were started and experiments with the rhythm method tried. The latter gave rise to much-told stories about the simple-mindedness of the village women and the naiveté of the experimenters, but led to few effective results. But a number of attitude surveys were made, and the findings convinced some government leaders that many in India would welcome family planning (S. Chandrasekhar 1953; Pathare 1966:47–48; K. Gould 1969b:1515, 1518).

Governmental expenditures for family planning rose steadily though not spectacularly until 1965. The program was given great new impetus in that year largely because some influential officials came to realize how greatly population growth hampered development advances. At the Cabinet level, strong leadership was given by C. Subramaniam, then Minister of Food and Agriculture, and by Asoka Mehta of the Planning Commission, later Minister of Planning. Enthusiasm for the new drive was stimulated by reports about the efficiency of the intrauterine contraceptive device, which seemed to offer a cheap, easy, reversible contraceptive method (Lewis 1970:15–17). Expenditures for family planning went from 65 million rupees in 1964–65 to 120 million the following year to 370 million (about 50 million dollars) in 1968–69; budgeted projections for the Fourth Five-Year Plan, 1969–74, provided for an annual average of about 600 million rupees; the actual expenditures were much less.

The organizational build-up was rapid. A United Nations evaluation mission surveyed India's family planning program in 1969 and reported that about 70,000 persons were then regularly employed in the program. They included 6,100 physicians and 35,500 paramedical workers. The mission commented appreciatively on the "impressive organizational set-up," which ranged from a special cabinet committee chaired by the Prime Minister down through every level of administration to the village council. The budgetary allocation in 1969 amounted to about one-tenth of one percent of the gross national product. This was as great or greater a per capita allocation as that of any governmental family planning program (UN 1969:10–29; also see Programme Evaluation 1970:16–29).

The effort to make people aware of family planning soon thrust itself on a visitor's notice everywhere in India. The symbol of the program, a red triangle with the apex down, was prominently posted in remote hamlets as well as along city streets. Posters bore the stylized, cheery depictions of four faces, parents and two children, with the slogan, "Two or three children, stop," or the later version, "Next child not yet, after the third, never." Newspapers frequently carried some mention of family planning, if nothing more than an advertisement for Nirodh ("protection") condoms, sold at low, subsidized prices. Family planning messages were often broadcast on the radio since a "family planning cell" was established in each of All-India Radio's principal stations. Cinema audiences were likely to be reminded of family planning in film shorts, news clips, or advertising slides. The message was also conveyed through traditional media of music, drama, and puppet shows. A large orchestration of all media was periodically assembled during a "gala family planning fortnight."

At one local fair I attended the family planning pavilion was crowded, the exhibits of the human reproductive organs attracting special interest. The physician in charge of the district program was at the exit to answer questions, and free samples of Nirodh were available. The national effort, as an advertising campaign, was thoughtfully and skillfully planned; one review of it said that it was "the largest public education effort ever undertaken by any nation" (Program Memorandum 1968:126; see also Wilder and Tyagi 1968).

By 1971 Dr. Agarwala could summarize estimates that about 80 percent of urban people and 60 to 70 percent of rural people were aware of modern family planning. Perhaps even more important was the new ease and frequency of discussion about family planning. S. Govind, in commenting on the increased practice of family planning, wrote, "The easy informality with which the subject of birth control, once a taboo, is being discussed today in our society, is a pointer in this direction" (Agarwala 1971:7; Govind 1970:25; Kale 1969:27). When Myron Weiner interviewed some ninety public leaders on the subject in 1969, few of them had a negative attitude and only four were actively opposed to the Family Planning Programme. The great majority thought it was important and urgently needed, but they also expressed a good deal of misinformation and lack of information about population matters. Weiner commented that "a program of popular education among India's leaders would appear to be called for" (1970:22–23). Village leaders also are likely to say that fertility control is a good thing for people and is needed by the nation, however much they may privately doubt its advisability for their own people and their own families.

With the greater use of contraceptives, production facilities were established in India. By 1970 there was a government factory for the production of intrauterine loops and another for condoms. A scheme for the distribution of condoms through the sales outlets of six large business firms floundered a bit, apparently because of bureaucratic delays (see Lewis 1970:24–25), but on the whole the production and distribution of contraceptive devices have been quite adequate for the demand. In these respects the drive since 1965 has been markedly successful. An administrative organization has been built up; the information campaign has been demonstrably effective; the ideological justification appears to be widely accepted; the industrial and distributional infrastructure is in place.

The Family Planning Programme: Achievements and Constraints

How successful, then, has the drive been in easing the burden of too many births? The national figures on the use of birth control methods are of considerable magnitude. By 1969 India accounted for more than half of all sterilization operations in the world (Presser 1970:11–12) and a sizable fraction of all IUD insertions. As of 1971, Agarwala estimated that about six million Indian couples in the reproductive years had limited their fertility through sterilization or IUD insertion; users of condoms and other contraceptive methods were estimated to be about two million couples. Agarwala concluded that "The couples currently protected in India appear to be around 8 million, or eight per cent of the reproductive couples." But he adds, "This is a far cry from the target of more than 90 per cent users" (1971:10). At the end of 1972 the Ministry of Health and Family Planning estimated that 13.44 million couples were "protected" by various methods, representing 13.3% of all Indian couples in the reproductive years (Report of Ministry 1972; also see Programme Evaluation 1970:6–7, 58). These numbers may give an unduly sanguine impression, since a good many of the IUDs inserted were soon extracted and many of those sterilized were probably older people who already had a large number of children. Nevertheless, these figures attest to the unceasing vigor of the governmental program.

However, the pay-off in lowered birth rates was not clearly apparent. On one page of an official brochure the estimate is given that 1.4 million births were prevented in 1968–69 through contraceptive methods; on a later page there is a note that about 13 million lives were added to the population that year (Department of Family Planning 1969:1, 7). The population increase of 24.7% during 1961–71 was the highest ever; the earlier increases by census decades were 11.00% in 1931, 14.23% in 1941, 13.31% in

1951, 21.64% in 1961 (Chandra Sekhar 1971:35). Although it may well have been too soon, at the time of the 1971 census, for the results of the post-1965 drive to have had perceptible impact, the year-by-year estimates did not give grounds for hope of rapid decreases. In 1965 the annual birth rate was estimated at 41 per thousand population and had been at that level for some two decades. For 1968 the national birth rate was estimated at 39.1, for 1969 at 38.8, and for 1971 at 37.1. There were lower estimates for certain states, such as 33.6 for the Punjab in 1968 and 1969 (Visaria 1971:1463–64; Lall 1973) and "below 32" in Kerala, Tamil Nadu, and Maharashtra, according to the Ministry of Health and Family Planning report for 1971–72 (Report of Ministry 1972). But progress toward the official goal of 25 per thousand for the nation was something less than swift. Moreover, even if this optimistic target were met, India's population would still increase by about 1%, say six million, per year. The United Nations Advisory Mission pointed out that if the population aims of the Fourth Plan were fulfilled, only one-third of the couples in the reproductive years would be protected through the Family Planning Programme (1969:15). Indian mothers would still be having their third child at an average age of 25 with a good many years of potential childbearing before them. Should the growth rate of 1961–71 continue, there would be as many people in India just a few decades into the twenty-first century as there were in the whole world at the beginning of the twentieth century. Agarwala estimates that at the 1961–71 rate, there will be one billion people in India by 1990. He supplies a note of small comfort: "If, however, family planning becomes successful, the billion mark may be reached 10–15 years later" (1971:8).

The report of the UN evaluation mission of 1969 gives similar, almost contradictory assessments, telling of quite good progress in the short term but indicating bafflement about prospects over the long term. John Lewis, former head of the United States AID Mission to India, said of the UN Report, "Given its rather remarkable ambivalence about a system that was doing rather well within its own terms of reference, but was also in process of missing its mark by a mile, the even more remarkable thing about the UN team is that it remained overwhelmingly congenial to the theory of the Indian program" (1970:21–22).

That theory, in Lewis' view, was based on some questionable assumptions. Certain clinical methods of contraception, notably IUD and sterilization, were emphasized, with less attention given to other modern methods and little or none to traditional methods. A large, complicated governmental organization was created, and this tended "to minimize involvement of private organizations, of gainfully motivated private medical practitioners (modern or traditional) and of commercial and market mechanisms. . . ." The program was placed within the public health bureaucracy, "in what, in the eyes of most observers, remains one of the weakest functional cadres in the Indian administrative system. . . ." Moreover, it was implied that once people heard about family planning, they would readily see that it was in their best interest and quickly begin to practice contraception; "the program assumed that there was no intransigent gap between private self-interest and public self-interest in the population field." There was, in the beginning stages, only modest experimentation with using money payments or other direct incentives (*ibid.:* 17–19).

The "philosophy behind the programme" was stated in 1968 by Dr. S. Chandrasekhar, the demographer who was then Union Minister of State with special responsibility for family planning. He pointed out that government agencies were to be much involved in encouraging family planning but that the actual regulation of births had to be left to voluntary adoption by couples and to the voluntary approval of their communities, "without offending their cultural, religious, and moral values and susceptibilities." An array of contraceptive methods would be available to all for voluntary selection (the "cafeteria approach" is the interesting term for this), with the presumption that, informed of the alternatives, a couple would be able to make the most rational choice available to them. The program, moreover, had to be an integral part of medical and public health services (1969:10–11).

The explicit policy and implicit assumptions of the Indian program were like those of most other national programs and showed the same shortcomings. Kingsley Davis has noted that the usual family planning program is not a program of effective fertility control at all. The efforts to make contraceptives conveniently available and their use popular do not reckon with the fact that users of contraceptives may still produce a fertility rate dangerous to their society. The number of children that couples want, whether in India or in many other countries, is not likely to be the number that the society should have if the people are to have the kind of life they also want for themselves and for their children. Davis cites data from India indicating that most of those who adopt contraceptive measures have already had more children than is compatible with the society's welfare. The usual family planning preference for rational, voluntary choice overlooks the fact that "what is rational in the light of a couple's situation may be totally irrational from the standpoint of society's welfare" (Davis 1967:733, 736–737; see also Polgar 1972:209).

The planners of these programs, Davis observes, tend to overmedicalize the control of conception. Most people who have deliberately reduced their fertility in the past have done so by simple methods that required few or no medical measures. Davis urges political leaders and population planners to move beyond the opening stages of their respective programs; "if it is only a first step, it should be so labelled and its connection with the next step (and the nature of that next step) should be carefully examined" (1967:737).

By the time of the 1971 Census, India's program was clearly ready for a next stage. Prime Minister Indira Gandhi had previously indicated some new directions. In addressing a family planning conference in 1969, she had said that the program's successes had been limited to only certain pockets of the population, mainly the more affluent, and that it was not reaching those who could most benefit from it. She pointed out the "danger of targetry," the bureaucratic inclination to set up quotas to be met, whether for sterilization or loop insertions or non-body counts. It is the inclination to concentrate on producing a proper set of figures rather than establishing a basis for real results. Her critique was supported by indications that there was as yet no apparent correlation between the intensity of the program's efforts in a particular region and the rate of population growth there (Program Memorandum 1968:22; Aiyar 1971; Misra 1973).

One of the most respected public figures in India, Jayaprakash Narayan, similarly warned that the drive would not succeed "if it remains only an official programme." He compared it to the over-officialized cooperative movement, of which he said, "It has not grown from below and no effort is being made to encourage the process of developing from below" (1968:14–15). One detailed assessment of the governmental program, whose author was then a "training associate in family planning," ascribed its shortcomings to a "topdown administrative bias which has ignored the social-cultural milieu of the rural Indian, which has pushed a program on a people who may not see its utility or purpose in their lives, which lacks sufficient or significant motivational research to determine how best to reach the rural Indian on a personal and not a target basis, and which is unable to capitalize on the existing successes with efficient extension or medical follow-up" (Humberger 1969:6).

Such strictures do not give sufficient recognition to the lively start that has been made and to the political and social constraints under which the planners worked. One difficulty was the pressure to show quick results even where real results would necessarily take a long time. A critic of Dr. Chandrasekhar's work as Minister charged that he had emphasized propaganda, patriotic appeals, and minor incentives rather than trying to shift basic motivations which must be altered if the program is to succeed (B. Dasgupta 1970:343–344). But while Dr. Chandrasekhar well understood the fundamentals of the problem as a demographer, as Minister he had also to understand the practical realities of the situation.

One of the most stubborn realities is noted by the critic himself. It is that in the Indian farmer's situation, having a large family is rational. Moreover, "it would be foolish to expect him, with no old age security, to risk having a small family" (ibid.: 344). Other observers have similarly pointed out that many villagers can see little or no gain to themselves from family planning and that village leaders find few rewards in it (Mencher 1970:38; Kamat 1971:724; Wyon and Gordon 1971:47). One observer concluded, on the basis of his study in villages near Baroda, that from the villagers' point of view, "the arguments of the government and other family planning workers did not make sense" (Poffenberger 1969:117–118). This contradiction between private interest and public welfare presents a formidable problem but is not necessarily a permanent obstacle in the way of effective reduction of the birth rate. There are also certain forces favorable to birth limitation, although information about them has not been abundantly available or systematically presented and has been overshadowed by a good deal of misinformation.

KAP Surveys: Guidance and Misguidance

The first plans were influenced by the results of questionnaire surveys of the existing knowledge, attitudes, and practices, called the KAP surveys. Literally hundreds of such studies were made in the 1950s and 1960s (see Agarwala 1962c; Kapil and Saksena 1968; Krishna Murthy 1968). Though they varied greatly in design, scope, and sample size, certain of the results were quite consistent. Thus the KAP findings, together with the results of action-research projects, showed that there should be a shift away from the rhythm and foam tablet methods toward a greater emphasis on sterilization and on efforts beyond the clinics (Program Memorandum 1968:27–30). Most importantly, the survey results encouraged officials to go ahead with increasing expenditures and helped imbue family planning workers with enthusiastic hope for their task. One finding was that most Indians were interested in learning about family planning. Although most were also quite ignorant of modern methods, they said that they were willing to learn how these methods were used. Relatively little opposition to family planning was evinced either on religious or on any other grounds. When asked how many children were ideal for a family, the respondents usually give a number decidedly smaller than the average number actually borne.

So it seemed from these surveys that very many people in India wanted to have fewer children than they were having and that they were willing to practice fertility limitation once they had the knowledge and means to do so. These conclusions, as it turned out, were unduly optimistic. Pilot projects later demonstrated that even when the relevant information was broadly disseminated to an experimental population among whom the means for contraception were made easily available, the proportion of those who actually limited the number of births by these means remained exceedingly small.

The Indian experience with KAP surveys and with the conclusions drawn from them was much like that of other developing countries. Philip Hauser, in a review of a book dealing with such studies in various countries, wrote that "it is a moot question whether surveys do not mislead as much as they inform." He noted that planners generally interpret "interest in learning" as indicating a favorable market for family planning. The usual surveys do not take sufficient account of what the questions mean to the respondent or whether he really has any significant answer to give. Hauser did acknowledge that the surveys could tap certain levels of information quite reliably and that the over-optimistic interpretations had nonetheless served usefully in persuading government officials to move in a desirable direction. He particularly commended the article by Dr. C. Chandrasekaran in which this demographer gave early warning about the interpretation of KAP surveys in India (Hauser 1967:403–404).

The manner in which survey workers elicited information was not always conducive to providing useful data. Commonly, for example, a village woman finds herself suddenly confronted by a young lady, carrying official-looking papers, who fires a series of questions at her. The village woman takes in the young lady's austerely elegant sari, her thin, expensive bangles, her carefully tended hair, smooth complexion, and her soft hand cleverly manipulating a ball-point pen. She is likely to give the kind of answers that she believes an educated person would like to hear.[2]

2. The unreliability of some responses was illustrated in Agarwala's study of six villages near Delhi, done in 1958–60. In that study 202 women (26.4% of the sample) and 149 men (42.6%) said that they had some knowledge of family planning methods; they were then asked to specify the methods they knew about. The "best-known" method, named by 28.8% of these women

The village woman may not quite understand some of the questions, especially when they are phrased in city language and spoken in a city accent. Some questions touch on intimate and perhaps sensitive aspects of her life. The sensitivity is not necessarily about discussing sex relations (see S. Chandrasekhar 1959: 70, Bogue 1962:538; Rao and Mathen 1970:81, 83). But when the questions deal with one's babies who have died or were born dead, or (perhaps worse) about never having conceived at all, then the answers may well be ways of averting such painful topics.

The question about the ideal size of a family is not a sensitive matter; the answers from the villagers give an average of four or five children, from townspeople about three children (cf. Krishna Murthy 1968:20). But if the interviewer can discuss the question with the respondent in any depth, he usually discovers that what is really considered ideal is to have at least two grown sons and a married daughter to provide support and comfort in one's later years. A computer study has shown that in the light of mortality rates and sex ratios, an Indian couple must bear six or seven children (6.3 on the average) in order to have 95% certainty that one son will survive to the father's sixty-fifth birthday. And that is just about the number, on the average, that they do have (Ridker 1969a:280–281; May and Heer 1968).

So in assessing the record and the potential of a family planning program, we must understand people's actual motivations, both for having many and for having fewer children. There are important variations, as we shall note, at different social, economic, and educational levels, but we must first consider the sentiments and experiences that are shared by the vast majority of India's people.

---

and 30.9% of the men, was that by "injections," a method that did not then exist in India. Perhaps some syringe operators did purport to give such injections, but it is likely, as the author writes, that the respondents guessed "that such a method must be existing in view of the widespread use of the injection by the medical practioners in India for various ailments" (1970:115).

PERSONAL MOTIVATIONS AND
CULTURAL CONSIDERATIONS

Why Large Families Are Wanted

ALMOST all young women marry, and are generally married relatively young. At her marriage a young wife can scarcely consider whether to limit the number of the children she will bear. The whole pressure of her husband's family, with whom she usually comes to live, and the expectations of her natal family, are that she will become pregnant as soon as possible and, having borne one child, will bear more. Typically a woman knows of no acceptable alternative role for herself than that of wife-mother. The dread possibility of being barren is a nightmarish specter for a woman who has not yet borne a child and becomes a painful reality for a childless older woman who finally must accept that she will never bear one. For all but a relative few, a woman's destiny lies mainly in her procreation; the mark of her success as a person is in her living, thriving children.

A young wife in a village is not encouraged to show any special interest in her husband in public, certainly not in any amorous way, but her husband's family nonetheless arranges matters so that the couple have opportunity for sexual relations, even in families where privacy is otherwise minimized and where elders keep the young wife under strict surveillance. In Sherupur, a village of Faizabad district, Uttar Pradesh, Ketayun Gould observed (1969:1889) that "rather than discourage contact, I have heard mothers-in-law goad their daughters-in-law in the hope that this will speed the production of an heir."

Once a woman becomes pregnant she is likely to receive more fond attention than she enjoys at any other time. At her first pregnancy, she is given a kind of respect in the household that she did not get before. During her subsequent pregnancies also, she usually gets favored treatment. Certainly for a young wife, pregnancy is fine, the baby is fun, motherhood is grand and God-given. Most of the religious rites in which a woman participates are intended for the welfare of her husband and children. Unless she has living children, her joys and status are the less, and so she prays fervently that her children may be many and healthy (see Opler 1964:211; Jacobson 1970:371–375).

Even a young woman is aware of the need to have children to care for her in her later years, if only from the pitiable example of those older women who are without living children and so are bereft of firm security in life and of soul's comfort after death. An elder woman's security lies principally in her sons. A daughter is far better for her than no child at all, but a daughter commonly leaves her parents' home at marriage and lives with her husband's family, usually in another village or part of town. An old woman who must rely on a son-in-law's bounty is not likely to be as comfortable as one who enjoys the unquestioned respect and support of her son.

Should a woman's husband be unable to sustain her or should he die, her grown sons are duty-bound to look after her. And many older women are so supported; one-half of Indian women aged 55–59 are without husbands (see Poffenberger 1968:764). Her sons, moreover, link a woman more securely with their lineage, the circle of close and close-living patrilineal kin who provide help in emergencies, solace in misfortune, shield against enemies. One young son is precious as an eye is precious, but a common saying has it that one eye is no eye and one son is no son (Opler 1964:207; Poffenberger 1969:86, 92). Child mortality is very high, and a woman should not have so much of her stakes in life wrapped up in only one small boy. The figures for infant mortality derived from successive rounds of the National Sample Survey give high rates; in the round of 1964–65 they were 127.29 infant deaths per thousand live births for the rural sample, and 79.39 for the urban sample (NSS Number 186, 1970:9).[1] But

1. Professor S. Chandrasekhar (formerly Minister of State) warns that these figures "must be taken with considerable reserve and caution." He

higher rates are reported from close studies of particular villages. Thus mothers in six villages of Delhi state had lost about 36% of their children within one year of birth (Agarwala 1970:119). In a village near Meerut, Uttar Pradesh, mothers under the age of 30 had already lost 38% of their live-born children. During the span of a year (1968–69), nearly a third of the children born to these villagers died within their first year of life (Marshall 1972b:28). In the Khanna area of the Punjab, the women who were over 44 years old had lost more than a third (37.2%) of the children they had borne. The authors of this study conclude that "until they have good assurance that live-born sons, and daughters, will survive, couples in the Khanna area are unlikely to be interested in restricting the numbers of their children beyond the present practice" (Wyon and Gordon 1971:139–140, 197–198, 205–206).

A woman whose children die in quick succession knows that she will be suspected of being a magnet for misfortune, and she tends to feel somehow personally culpable. She becomes all the more anxious to redeem herself by bearing children who will live. Especially does she keep trying to produce sons. A woman who has borne only daughters is usually determined to make yet another attempt for a son, no matter what the personal risk. "No sons beget many children" is an apt popular saying. The ideal number of children as three or four, so commonly given in KAP survey reports, should be understood to mean, as has been mentioned, at least two healthy, grown sons and one daughter suitably married (Mysore 1961:143; Pathare 1966:55; Kaur and Edlefson 1968:14; Kale 1969:18; Poffenberger 1969:87, 99; Mamdani 1972:132, 140).

---

notes that the National Sample Survey, set up in 1951 by the Ministry of Finance of the Government of India and the Indian Statistical Institute, has made annual rounds in which respondents were interviewed about certain subjects. The samples were drawn from about a thousand villages, fifty towns, and four cities. Professor Chandrasekhar says that the limitations of this interview method "in Indian conditions where the person interviewed is under no obligation to answer, much less to the best of his or her knowledge, are obvious" (1972:141). This caveat is justified, but the NSS findings are nevertheless worth using as reflections of broad relations, general trends, and approximate magnitudes.

A man feels the same strong desire for children as does his wife, though his reasons are a bit different and are differently weighted (see Mysore 1961:146–157; Poffenberger 1969:83; Marshall 1972a:337–340). He can scarcely attain full manly estate and dignity unless he has children. He too is mindful of support for his later years, but, in addition, he has a pressing practical need for sons in his middle years. If he is a farmer, he is likely to want help with the daily chores and to need help badly at harvest time and at other periods of labor shortage. He knows that the costs of raising a son are little as compared with the physical help and general benefits that a youngster can give. Artisans have the same views about having sons; laborers know that even a youngster may bring home wages that can make a considerable difference in the house.

The great economic advantage of having many children is shown in Mahmood Mamdani's reports of interviews he conducted in the village he calls Manupur, one of seven test villages covered by the Khanna study. That project was an intensive demographic investigation of villagers near the market town of Khanna in the Ludhiana district of Punjab state. The study covered about 8000 people in the test population and 8000 in the control population. Planned by members of the Harvard School of Public Health in collaboration with Indian government agencies, the field work started in 1953 and ended in 1969; the most intensive period of data collection was 1954–60. Mamdani, who was not connected with the project but was given access to the records, conducted his interviews in the summer of 1970, and has written a sharply critical assessment of the Khanna study.

One part of the project as it was planned was to persuade couples in the test villages to adopt modern methods of fertility control. This attempt was not successful, and Mamdani criticizes the planners for failing to understand the economic rationality of bearing numerous children and the irrationality, to the villagers, of trying to curtail their numbers. Men from every social and economic level in Manupur village, with only a few exceptions, testified to the economic value of children, especially of sons. Farmers who have little land, five acres or less, cannot afford to hire any outside labor and have to rely on the family for all their labor requirements. Economic improvement for these men can come about only through increasing the family labor force. Every one of the 49 men of this group (37% of the 131 farmers interviewed by Mamdani) "expressed the hope that with a large enough family—especially with one spaced close together—a few children could be spared to live away from the family land, thus accumulating some savings and perhaps buying more land, land which could be worked with the manpower available within the family itself" (Mamdani 1972:76).

The landless laborers of Manupur are mainly of the lowest jatis, and their employment is largely seasonal. The women and girls as well as the men and boys earn wages during the times of high labor demand. For them, a larger family means greater income during the busy season and thus greater savings for the slow season. The artisan and other service groups also want to have enough children to accumulate savings and so to be able to lift themselves out of constant debt and penury (ibid.:95, 115). "And so, in Manupur, those who had few resources responded to adversity not by decreasing their numbers, but by increasing them. In numbers they found security and the only opportunity for prosperity" (ibid.:127).

During the years when the Khanna study was being conducted, crop yields in this village, as well as in the district and state generally, rose sharply as a result of introduced improvements in agricultural technology. Ludhiana district was one of those selected for the experimental Intensive Agricultural Development Program. The villagers of Manupur were able to intensify their farming practices, with consequent increases in the work load as well as in the wheat harvest. And the economic benefits contributed by the work of a farmer's children were even greater in this part of the state than elsewhere (ibid.:77, 90).

The wealthier farmers of Manupur, those who own 17 or more acres of cultivated land, can afford the machines which reduce their need for field hands. But the fourteen men of this prosperous class have not tried to reduce the size of their families, partly because they continue to believe that a man's best and greatest assets are his sons and partly because they are not sure about the long-term effects of the new technology (*ibid.*:84–87).

Because this new and very lucrative kind of farming requires new technical skills and increased dealings with officials, the villagers have an added incentive to educate their children. They feel that at least one son should be educated through high school. The only way in which a poor family can afford to educate a son is to have several so that one can be supported by the others while he is going to school. This has worked well for a number of Manupur families. In one barber family with five sons, the three eldest have supported each other through college, and the father expects the two younger to be similarly supported by their elder brothers (*ibid.*:101, 116).

Many in India share these views about having children, believing that the more sons they have, the greater the family's chances for economic gains. Those who are concerned about their children's education commonly reckon, as do the men in Manupur, that if they have several sons some of them will help pay for the education of the others. Those who find that they may have more sons than their land or trade can support hopefully expect that some will find jobs elsewhere and return part of their wages to the family purse. All know that a flourishing set of sons provides insurance in case of sickness, credit against debt, and the best kind of strength to meet social obligations.

Other practical considerations impel a villager to want as many sons as he can muster. Factional quarrels are endemic in many villages (see Mandelbaum 1970:240–264, 373–380). Only a large, united cohort of sons and brothers can be confident of holding their own against the depredations and denigrations that men can expect to face. When villagers of Ludhiana district discussed birth control with research workers of the Khanna project, they told of the bitter village rivalries and put the matter pointedly: "These fights are won by men, not by contraceptives" (Wyon and Gordon 1971:231; Mamdani 1972:133:136).

Men and women find their need for children repeated and reinforced in religion. Hindu scripture teaches that a man remains in debt to his ancestors until he produces a son; that a son can save his father's soul from a terrible fate in the afterworld, especially by performing the memorial rites called *sraddh* (see Pathare 1966:54; R. W. Taylor 1969:8–10; Tripathi 1969:71–73). An act of lesser importance than raising a son, but still of high religious merit, is the giving of a daughter in marriage. Islam and the other principal religions of India similarly encourage the bearing of children, though in other terms and through different rites.

Yet the effect of religion on fertility has been both overemphasized and underrated. It has been overemphasized in that the memorial rites can be performed by a surrogate son. These rites, moreover, are not of imperative consequence among many of India's people, especially among the poorest. Another kind of misinterpretation is the frequent mention that neither Hinduism nor Islam specifically forbids the practice of contraception. This may be true enough now, but once birth planning becomes a matter of strong political contention, it will not be difficult for opponents to find scriptural justification for their opposition.

Nor is the presumed fatalism of Indian peoples a weighty factor. True enough, questions put to villagers and townspeople about birth limitation often elicit the response, "It is in God's hands" or "It is God's will." But this is mainly a way of saying that the respondent feels that he has no knowledge or power to affect the situation or that he is afraid to take certain measures (Poffenberger and Poffenberger 1972:29). Once a person learns that he can safely exert some influence on the outcome of an event, he is likely to alter his idea of the Karma, the immutable fate, involved in it. Ketayun Gould tells that women in the village of Sherupur did not know about modern contraceptive methods. "Thus, 'it is in God's hands' is to be rightly translated as 'there is always a risk of pregnancy once you have sexual relations' and not as a passive-defeatist attitude" (Gould 1969:1891). This is true throughout India; people typically do their utmost to improve their social status and their material lot when they can. The idea of *Karma* has not precluded social competition or economic striving but is rather used to express the limitations within which efforts for self-improvement can be waged (see Kolenda 1964; Mandelbaum 1970:412, 429–430).

What is usually slighted in discussion of religion and fertility is the deeper power of a person's religion, the ways in which it gives formal, effective expression to motives that rise out of his whole life experience. Such motives stem from the common human condition as well as from the particular life problems scheduled by his culture. A universal human quandary, one that is likely to strike a man as he comes into his middle years, is the dilemma of death, of ceasing to be. Each religion followed in India prescribes its special ways of defeating death, but adherents of all find in their sons a sure means of prolonging something of one's self beyond the mortal span. The rites performed by a man's sons are external expressions that help meet this common internal desire.

In all, a person's family is a major focus of his life expectations and activities. Children are one's chief source of lasting pleasure and prime goal of affection; they are the means of attaining respected status, the avenue for creativity and achievement. Judith Blake has portrayed the strong reason for having children in Western societies (1965:60); they are all the more true for most Indians, whose culture, religion, and livelihood alike require that a man and woman raise several children to fulfill their aspirations. No special decision is required to have and to keep having children. Each spouse only follows the course that biological urge, cultural expectation, social approval, and practical advantage indicate. What does require firm decision is to avert or delay conception.

Motivations for Controlling Fertility: Birth Spacing

Despite the pressures for having children, a number of people in India traditionally made the decision to limit fertility directly or indirectly. And they did so before modern contraceptive methods were known. Married women in India have in recent decades borne an average of about 6.6 children during their entire reproductive period, between the ages of 15 and 45 (Agarwala 1966a:94–96; 1966b:797). Much higher average numbers of live births have been reported for other large populations; the small group of Hutterites in the United States and Canada achieved a notable average of 10.6 (see Wrigley 1969:17). The annual birth rate in India has recently been about 40 per thousand population; Guatemala showed a birth rate of 49 during 1954–58 (Wyon and Gordon 1971:152). Some part of the lower fertility figures for Indian women may be ascribable to generally poorer nutrition and health, but some part is also the result of deliberate birth limitation.

The impact of traditional controls is reflected in the Khanna study, where the authors report that fertility in the whole sample was about 40 births per thousand per year (37.7 during 1957–59) instead of a readily obtainable 55; the wealthier, higher-ranking caste groups had much lower fertility than that of poorer groups. "That some birth control was practiced, and effectively, is indicated by a crude birth rate among leather workers of 51 per 1000 persons per year, 34 among farmers, and 31 for other high castes." The latter two groups made up 62% of the population studied. One aim of this study, as we have noted, was to introduce modern contraceptive methods and to test their effectiveness. The tests showed very little effect of the introduced methods, but the authors concluded that the villagers, in their traditional ways, "practiced appreciably more birth control than originally supposed" (*ibid.*:15, 152, 236, 311).

Other studies of fertility in India also indicate that at some time in their married lives, normally after several of their offspring have survived early childhood, many men and women in India begin to think about trying to postpone the birth of another child or to stop having children entirely. If one or both of them are inclined to try for control, the decision may develop without any spoken agreement between them. One simple way of trying to limit births is by stricter observance of customary taboos on sexual relations during certain periods. Other traditional methods range from those that are quite ineffective (dependence on a false "safe period") to one that is totally effective (total abstinence). The use of modern contraceptive methods has begun to be of some significance only in recent years.

Lists of all the possible reasons for fertility limitation by Indian couples present an imposing array (see Bogue 1962; Humberger 1969; Mysore 1961:143–156). But such lists say little about the effectiveness of each motive. And effective motivation is the central factor in fertility control. Techniques for doing so are not unimportant, especially as modern contraceptive means become readily available, but the primary factor is a person's strong desire to limit her and his fertility (see Kar 1968). One Indian medical man wrote, in objecting to the Family Planning Programme's emphasis on technical methods rather than on motivation, "In a group of willing people, *any* method will do the trick" (Dheer 1964:1503). Actually, only a few of the possible reasons for limiting fertility have been significantly effective.

One strong reason is to protect the health of child and mother through a proper spacing of births. Many people believe that the well-being of both is endangered if the next birth comes too quickly. Hence a postpartum taboo on intercourse is observed in almost all groups in India, though the stipulated length of the taboo period varies considerably, from just a few months to two years and more. One of the longest taboo periods reported is from Senapur, a village near Benares, whose people say that a couple should stop having intercourse when the woman becomes pregnant and that the period of abstention should continue for two years after childbirth. They believe that the health of a nursing child is impaired if the mother becomes pregnant again before the child is weaned. In one case in which the child was two-and-a-half years old when its next sibling was born, "the family was roundly criticized throughout the village" (Opler 1964:218). Although some couples may honor the full taboo period as much in the breach as in the observance, such standards are likely to affect the birth rates. A two-year postpartum abstention is regarded as desirable in Khalapur village in western Uttar Pradesh (Minturn and Hitchcock 1966:144). Even when the postpartum taboo period is much shorter, closely spaced pregnancies are commonly deprecated. Thus in a study of several Bengal villages, Mathen notes that "jokes are made when a woman becomes pregnant very frequently and there are special words to denigrate a woman who delivers every year for a number of years" (1962:44). In Tamil there is a term, *savali*, for a child whose younger sibling has been born soon after his birth (Mysore 1961:137).

Survey questions about birth spacing commonly yield replies that an interval of three to four years is desirable (R. Gupta 1965:5; Kurtkoti 1970:12; Programme Evaluation 1970:45, 155), though few respondents name a taboo period long enough to guarantee such spacing. Thus in the Mysore study the respondents said that the period of abstention should be about a year, though the sample of 739 city men gave a lower median of 33 weeks and rural women (353) a higher median of 61 weeks. On the proper interval between successive births, rural and city women gave a median answer of about 3.66 years (44 months); the median answers given by rural men was 35 months, and by city men 33.5 months (Mysore 1961:137–139). The inquiry did not probe into the discrepancy between the recommended taboo period of about a year and the desirable birth interval of some three years and more. It may well be that these respondents shared the commonly held belief that a woman is not likely to conceive again while she is breast feeding a child.

An interval of three to four years has been achieved among some groups. Thus 3.8 years was the average interval between births reported in a sample of 2469 women of Nagpur district in Madhya Pradesh. For these women the mean interval between their first and second births was 4.1 years, that between their third and fourth births 3.5 years (Driver 1963:76). Average intervals of more than three years have also been reported from other studies: 3.01 years from a sample of 113 Brahmin women of Nagpur city (Rakshit 1962:151); about 3.1 years from a survey of 1846 village women of Athoor block in Tamil Nadu (K. Srinivasan 1967:58); 3.2 years for women of a middle-class Delhi ward (Thapar 1965: 142). Other surveys report average intervals of about two and a half years (Mysore 1961:138; Agarwala 1970:97–98). A marked shortening of birth intervals seems to have occurred in recent decades. Rural women who had been married before 1941 showed an average interval of 40.80 months in a large nationwide sample; those married after 1941 averaged 33.47 months. The comparable figures for the samples of urban women were 37.60 and 30.97 months (NSS Number 154, 1970:13–14).

The Khanna study provides one test of villagers' belief that a woman is not likely to conceive while she is breast feeding her child. The average birth interval reported was about 30 months and, according to this research, a factor in the spacing is that lactation delays the resumption of ovulation and menstruation by an average of 10 months. Before that resumption, a woman has relatively little chance of becoming pregnant, even though the postpartum period of abstinence in the Khanna area is only about 4 months. Only 7% of the conceptions recorded in the study occurred before the woman resumed ovulation and had any postpartum menstruation. Once she begins menstruating again, breast feeding makes little difference in the incidence of her next pregnancy. Nearly all these mothers nursed their children and continued the nursing for an average of two years (Wyon and Gordon 1971:158, 168–169).[2]

In the Khanna area there was an average period of about 10 months between resumption of menstruation and next conception, the interval being longer for the older mothers and the interval between birth and the next conception much shortened if

2. Breast feeding continued for an average period of 22.6 months among a sample of 886 women in villages of Lucknow district, Uttar Pradesh. These were women who had borne children in 1963 and 1964. By the time the data collection was ended in September 1966, 14% of these women were still nursing; their average period of lactation at that date had been about 36.5 months. Although the average period of postpartum amenorrhea in this whole sample was 12.5 months, it was less for the younger women: 8.8 months in age group 15–19; 11 months in age group 20–24. In this study too, it was found that very few women became pregnant before resuming menstruation; the data seemed to show that in the period after a woman resumed menstruation and while she was still breast feeding the child, there was a low incidence of conception (Seghal and Singh 1967; also see Dandekar 1959:62, Jain 1967b:385; Rao and Mathen 1970:54; Oberg 1971; Raphael 1972). This may be a result of a lower incidence of coitus because of the belief that a nursing mother's milk becomes "spoiled," or at least less good for the child, after she has intercourse.

the infant died in its first month or was still-born. In the latter
cases the average length of postpartum amenorrhea was 2 months,
and the average period of abstinence only 2.2 months (Potter *et al.*
1965b:390–395; Wyon and Gordon 1971:160).

The intervals between pregnancies here may have been additionally lengthened because a woman in this region usually goes
to her parental home (which is always in another village and
where she must not have intercourse with her husband) for her
first birth and remains there for months. Of the first births recorded in the Khanna study, 80% took place away from the husband's home. After her first childbirth a woman is less likely to go
to her parents to give birth; the proportions of those who did so
were 36% for second deliveries, 24% for third, 15% for fourth,
and 5% for higher-order births. These decreasing visits may be
the reason for the longer average interval, of 33.1 months, between
first and second births, as against 31.3 months between the second
and third births (Wyon and Gordon 1971:157). But in the country
generally, such visits are a minor factor in lengthening birth intervals as compared with the continued effects of lactation and of
postpartum sexual abstinence. Indeed, a study of postpartum
abstinence among a sample of married women in Bombay revealed that more than half had abstained for a longer period than
that stipulated by the "customary taboo" of their social group.

The study included 1510 women, living in four wards of Bombay city, who had borne live children during January–March
1965. Interviews with them were held shortly after their confine-
ments and were repeated later. By the time the collection of data
ended in 1966, 67.1% of them said that they had resumed sexual
relations. Their mean period of postpartum abstinence was 14.64
weeks, not much longer than the average given by the couples in
the Khanna study. But nearly a third of the Bombay women (497)
had not yet resumed sexual relations at the time of the last interview, and some of these couples presumably abstained for a full
year or more. One of the questions asked of these women in the
first interview was about the "customary taboo," presumably
meaning the traditional period of abstinence that might apply to
them. From information gathered in later interviews with 1105 of

the women, it turned out that 14% of them had resumed sexual relations before the time they had given, 33% had observed just that period, but 53% had abstained for a longer period than they had stipulated as customary (Karkal 1971:21–26). A possible inference is that slightly more than half the women and their husbands had lengthened the customary period of taboo in order to postpone the birth of their next child.

In some groups couples achieve an average interval of three to four years between births and in other groups considerably less, but it is clear that the longer interval is the commonly desired one. Ketayun Gould emphasizes that this preference is strong among the villagers she knows and that a health worker should therefor "choose such moments when it is known that there is fear of an unwanted pregnancy to suggest the possibility of using contraceptives for *spacing purposes*" (1969a:1890).

Motivations for Controlling Fertility: The Pregnant Grandmother Complex

Another motive for curtailing fertility is commonly felt by a wife and husband in the later years of the wife's child-bearing period. A woman whose children are old enough to be having children of their own may feel herself demeaned if she becomes pregnant again, particularly if there is a daughter-in-law in the house. A good many villagers hold that marital sexual relations should be minimized or, ideally, abandoned once the need for procreation has been met. Thus in a study of a village in eastern Uttar Pradesh, such a woman is reported to feel disgrace; in an account of a village in central Uttar Pradesh, she is said to have a "feeling of shame." "Cutting jokes" about such women are made in a Bengal village, and the Mysore study mentions "community criticism" (Opler 1964:218; Gould 1969:1890; Mathen 1962:44; Mysore 1961:133).[3] Almost all the relevant studies show fertility

3. From her study of Nimkhera village in Madhya Pradesh, Doranne Jacobson notes (in a personal communication) that "The few women who had babies while their children were having babies were not criticized." In this village older women were not ashamed of being sexually active. This is quite contrary to the situation in almost all other Indian villages from which this matter has been reported. Also see footnote 8, page 38.

curtailment in the women's later years but usually less among the poorer and lower-status groups than among the wealthier and better educated.

This contrast is clearly demonstrated in a study done in 1947–49 (Chandrasekaran and George 1962). Three samples of Bengali Hindu women were taken from villages (1542 in the sample), from a middle-class section of Calcutta (1308), and from an upper-class part of the city (1448). The people of the villages, some twenty miles from Calcutta, were mainly agriculturists and poor; literacy among the women was 11%. The middle-class Beniatola section was inhabited by families whose occupations were mainly in small trade and lower-paying clerical positions; here the women's literacy rate was 84%. Ballygunge was the residence of wealthier families; most of the men were in highly paid professions, and 97% of the women were literate, with an extraordinarily high proportion (13%) of the married women having completed a college education.

Fertility was highest among the village women. The authors calculated that at the completion of their reproductive periods the village women would have had an average of 7.3 live births, the middle-class women 6.2, and the upper-class women 5.7. The research workers explored the possibility that the difference was due to the earlier effective marriage of the village women, 12.6 years. The comparable average age for the middle-class women was 14.7, and for the upper-class women 16.9 years. But the village women took much longer after marriage to produce their first child than did the others, presumably because of adolescent infertility. The difference in average age at first birth (16.5 years, 17.2, and 17.8) showed a spread of only 1.3 years, as compared with the spread of 4.3 years in average age at effective marriage (*ibid.*:74). Moreover, the city women caught up with the village women after several years, so that the age of a mother at the birth of her fourth child was virtually the same in all three groups. Village women over 35 in the study had borne their fourth child at an average age of 25.0, exactly the same average age as the Ballygunge women at fourth-order birth; the comparable figure for the Beniatola women was 25.2 years. So the earlier age at effective marriage of the village women did not account for their higher fertility.

What did help explain the fertility differential was the average age at termination of last pregnancy. For the village women it was 35.4, for Beniatola 33.1, for Ballygunge 32.7 years. The village women had continued having children for an average of 2.7 years longer than did the upper-class city women. This study did not inquire why the city women stopped earlier, and the brief inquiries about how they did so did not yield clear answers. Yet, even in the village, the average age at termination of last pregnancy for currently married women aged 40–44 was 35.4 years, considerably short of their full reproductive potential.

Similar findings were reached in the Khanna study, where the women of the dominant, wealthier group of landowning Jats bore significantly fewer children on the average than did the poorer women of the Chamar leatherworkers and laborers, even though no significant differences were found in birth intervals or in contraceptive practices (Potter et al. 1965a:198–199). Among the woman aged 45 or more and currently married, the Jat women (226 in the sample) had borne an average of 7.0 live births; Chamar women (108) had borne 8.2. Here also, the women of higher and wealthier status stopped having children sooner. Jat women were, on the average, 36.3 years old at their last live birth, the Chamar 38.2 years. Since even this latter figure is below the biological potential, the authors conclude that some kind of fertility control is used by these villagers in the later years of a wife's reproductive span. They estimate that it is "probably a consequence of infrequent coitus, practice of birth control, and a developing physiological sterility" (Wyon and Gordon 1971:162, 169; Potter et al. 1965a:198).

The same kind of fertility limitation is reflected in a 1956 survey of 2380 couples in villages near Banaras. The couples were grouped in four categories according to caste and occupational status: Hindus of higher, intermediate, and lower categories, and non-Hindus (virtually all Muslims). In all four categories, women married for 10 to 14 years had borne nearly the same average number of children; 3.54 for the higher and 3.44, 3.43, 3.16 for the three other classes in order. But for the women married for 30 years or more (who had thus completed their reproductive periods or very nearly so), there were marked differences. The higher-status women ended their reproductive years with significantly fewer births, evidently because they had stopped bearing children sooner. The average number of their births was 5.74, as compared with 7.57 for the intermediate class, 6.93 for the lower, and 7.57 for the Muslims (Rele 1963:185).

More precise evidence on age at termination of childbearing comes from two small samples of high-status city women. One study, done in 1959, covered 103 Maharashtrian Brahmin women in Nagpur city. All were over 45 or had reached the menopause; each had lived with her husband through her entire reproductive span. The average number of births was 6.06, and the mean age at last birth (for 89 of the women) was 33.37 years. Ninety of the women could give reasonably approximate dates for the onset of their menopause, yielding a mean age at menopause of 45.84 years. For 77 women who could give particularly accurate datings, the mean interval between last birth and menopause onset was 12.46 years (Rakshit 1962:144–151).

The other study, done in Calcutta about 1950, included 93 women over 45 years of age from relatively affluent families of Brahmin, Vaidya, and Kayastha caste affiliations. Almost all were literate and generally quite precise about the relevant dates in their reproductive histories. Their average number of births was high, 7.85,[4] even though the mean age at last birth was 35.10 years. The mean interval between last birth and menopause for these women was 12.41 years (T. Sen 1953:49–54). These Calcutta women and those in the Nagpur sample managed, on the average, to avert childbirth for more than a dozen years before their menopause. They did so with little or no use of modern contraceptive devices or sterilization procedures, although abortion was a considerable factor, as we shall note later, in the Nagpur sample.

In sum, women of wealthier, higher-status families tend to stop

4. The high average of births, 7.8, reported for the affluent women of this Calcutta sample contrasts with the mean of 5.7 births reported from a much larger sample interview in 1948–49, of similarly affluent women in Calcutta (Chandrasekaran and George 1962:87).

having children at an earlier age, according to the relevant studies, than do women of lower status. They also have a lower average number of children borne, although there are some notable exceptions.[5] Children of wealthier familes, as we shall note below, have a much higher rate of survival. Ill and ill-nourished women may not be able to bear children for as many of their years as do healthy women, but in India it is generally the women of the better nourished groups who stop earlier. Their motivations seem to rise as much from an excess of shame as from a sufficiency of children.

Fertility Reduction Because of Widowhood

Two indirect means of limiting fertility are of special interest. One is the ban on widow remarriage, a factor that is now diminishing in demographic importance; the other is the modern trend to marry girls at a later age than was traditionally thought proper, a factor of increasing importance.

Widow remarriage is prohibited mainly among those who maintain the standards of the three highest scriptural categories, the "twice-born" varnas of Brahmins, Kshatriyas, and Shudras (see Mandelbaum 1970:78, 223). But this ban is not observed among most of India's people, and a young widow of other caste groups has a good chance of being remarried, especially if she has only one or two children at her husband's death. There was a remarriage rate of 89.1% (41 of 46) for women in a Nagpur district sample who had been widowed before age 25; but only 8.1% (3 of 37) for women in the sample who had been widowed between the ages of 35 and 44 (Driver 1963:78). A sample survey of villagers in three districts near Delhi showed that some 80% of the women who were widowed between the ages of 15 and 19,

5. In the Khanna study 50 women of the "Brahman and commercial" classification, aged 45 and over, had produced an average of 8.1 live births, close to the 8.2 mean for the Chamar women (Wyon and Gordon 1971:140). In the Mysore study wealthier women in villages and towns had a higher fertility rate than did women of poorer groups, though the differences were not large (Mysore 1961:87, 128). There were also only small fertility differences among caste categories in the survey of six villages near Delhi; women of the Jats and allied groups had somewhat lower fertility in their later years than did Brahmin or Chamar women (Agarwala 1970:100).

remarried, and the same proportion of childless widows, of whatever age, remarried. Only about 5% of those widowed between
ages 35 and 39 remarried, and only about 10% of widows with
four children remarried (Agarwala 1967a:134). Agarwala points
out that the remarriage of widows is practically assured among
several caste groups in this region because of their custom of the
levirate, in which one of a deceased man's brothers (either an unmarried or an already married man) is expected to take his widow
as wife directly after her mourning period is over (1966a:85–90;
1967a:131).[6] Among the people covered in the Khanna study, well
over half belonged to groups that honor the levirate; only about
6% were from groups in which quite the opposite custom, of for-
bidding widow remarriage, is followed. In the whole Khanna
sample, 60% of those widowed before the age of 35 had been remarried (Wyon and Gordon 1971:164–165).

Some widows who could remarry choose not to do so. If a
widow has young children, especially if they are boys, their rights
to their father's land may be jeopardized if their mother remarries
and moves away. Their land is then held for them by a patrilineal
kinsman who may manipulate affairs so that he obtains legal
possession before the boys come of age. If the widowed mother
stays in the village and manages the land, she and her sons are far
more sure of keeping it (see Jacobson 1970:229).

Our principal question here is by how much the condition of
widowhood keeps fertile women from having children; that is, in
what degree does it lower average fertility. Kingsley Davis esti-

6. Commonly coupled with the levirate in northern India is the custom of
permitting sexual relations between a married woman and her husband's
younger brothers. This is allowed on the grounds that such intimacy is all
in the interest of the family and will facilitate the transfer of full conjugal
relations if the elder brother should die (Mandelbaum 1970:64–66). This
practice is known among the groups that made up a part of the sample in
the Khanna study and may help explain the extraordinarily low rate of
primary sterility, about 1% among women in that sample (Wyon and
Gordon 1971:165–166). The low sterility rate may thus represent the effects
of female sterility only, not that of male and female combined, as in most
statistics on sterility, since the fraternal sharing may cancel out the effects of
a husband's sterility. About a fifth of the men over 25 in the total sample remained unmarried (*ibid.*:94, 96, 251).

mated that the ban on widow remarriage curtailed the Hindu birth rate, in the period 1901–1941, by an average of 16.4%. If and when those who upheld this taboo discarded it, he wrote, the already high fertility rate would go up even higher (1946:253; 1951:80–82; also see Mysore 1961:113; Agarwala 1964:76). By the 1970s, however, the demographic effects of this ban had been considerably modified, even among those who still cherished it. Indian men are now living longer than they used to, so that the average duration of marriage has markedly lengthened. Agarwala finds that in the decade 1931–41, Indian women on the average lost 8.0 years of fertile union because of the incidence of widowhood; this was 23.0% of the total mean length of fertile unions (calculated to woman's age 50). By the decade 1951–61, this loss had been reduced to an average of 1.9 years, or 5.5% of the mean duration (1968:14; also see Bhate 1964). The incidence of widowhood thus still has some effect in lowering the general fertility rate, though it is far less than it used to be.

Not only are longer-lived men creating fewer young widows in the "twice-born" groups that traditionally barred widow remarriage, but the age of marriage in these groups has been rising, and few of their girls now have their wedding before puberty. So the number of girls widowed before their marriages have been consummated, and so consigned to lifelong celibacy, has greatly diminished. Moreover, some of their young, childless widows are now married again quietly, with the previous marriage quickly and conveniently glossed over, if not completely forgotten (see Jacobson 1970:375). In all, the taboo on widow remarriage seems to have become quite a minor factor in contemporary fertility rates.

Fertility Reduction Because of Rise of Age at Nuptials

The ongoing rise in the average age of women at marriage, however, is likely to be a factor of considerable importance. In considering this, we should be aware of the distinction between a girl's age at her wedding ceremony and at the beginning of her marital sexual relations. A girl who is married before puberty does not customarily begin living with her husband until after her first menstruation. Then a nuptial ceremony, called *gauna* in Hindi, is celebrated for the couple, and after that they begin regular sexual relations. When a girl is married several years after her menarche, the two rites are usually celebrated together, though in a few such marriages some months elapse between the wedding and the nuptial ceremonies (cf. Karkal 1968:52, Table II). The time of the nuptial rites marks the consummation of the union; it is the date of "effective marriage."

Another relevant consideration is that of adolescent infertility. The human female does not develop into full reproductive maturity for several years after her first menstruation. During those years there is, on the average, significantly less chance of conception than there is after the age of 19 or 20. So Indian women who begin their effective marriage soon after their first menstruation have a longer average interval between effective marriage and first birth than do women who marry later (Mandelbaum 1954; Montagu 1957; Mysore 1961:116; Agarwala 1966a:105). We have already noted this factor in the study of women from two sections of Calcutta and from the Singur villages. The average age at effective marriage for the village women was 12.6 years, for the high-status Ballygunge women 16.9, a difference of 4.3 years. But the average age at first birth was 16.5 years in Singur, 17.8 years in Ballygunge, a difference of only 1.3 years (Chandrasekaran and George 1962:74; Talwar 1965).

Women who begin their effective marriage at the earliest ages do produce, on the average, a greater number of children, but the earlier time of effective marriage appears, on analysis, to be more a clue to other high-fertility practices than it is a major reason for the higher fertility. It is true that, if the average age at effective marriage were raised high enough, there would be an appreciable decline in fertility rates. But a rise from, say, average age 15 to 16 would not diminish births by very much. Using the Calcutta–Singur data, Talwar calculated that at age 15, 40% of the married women in the sample were nonfecund; at age 16, 29% were still nonfecund. The decline continued in the three later years; by age 17, 22% were not yet fecund, by age 18, 9%, and by age 19, none (Talwar 1965:259).

If the mean age at effective marriage for all Indian women were raised from 16.8 to age 20.5, according to a computer simulation, the birth rate would be reduced by 23% after 20 years. Agarwala estimates that if the minimum age at marriage for women were actually 20, the eventual decrease in the Indian birth rate would be about 30% (1966b:798). Other demographers have reached lower estimates, of 15 or 16% reduction, for the same calculation (Talwar 1967:294; Chidambaram 1967). These, we must note, are interesting mathematical calculations, not assessments of political feasibility or social potential.

Even at that, fertility rates in Kerala seem to challenge these estimates. Women in Kerala, Agarwala notes (1966b:798), marry at about an average age of 20 [7] and yet produce as many children as do Punjabi women who marry at an average age of about 17.5 years. But, he adds, what is constant throughout India is that, within each region or group, those women who marry markedly later than the average age at effective marriage for their group have significantly fewer children than do those who marry earlier. In most parts of India, those groups in which the age at effective marriage of girls is raised to 20 and above will do a good deal to lower their birth rates (Agarwala 1966a:104–107; 1967b:38–41, 132–134; 1970:107).

On the national average, the ages of girls at wedding and at effective marriage have increased markedly in recent decades. Between the Census of 1921 and that of 1961 the average age of women at marriage (wedding) increased by 1.94 years, from 13.89 to 15.83 years. The rise in average age at effective marriage was 1.12 years, from 15.29 to 16.41, as reported by rural women in a National Sample Survey covering a comparable period (pre-1921

7. Agarwala's estimate seems to be high. An analysis of the 1961 Sample Census gives average age at marriage in Kerala as 18.5 years for rural women and 19.1 for urban women (Namboodiri 1968:52). Another analysis of the 1961 Census for Kerala showed 18.6 years for rural women and 19.0 years for urban women (Jain 1967a:26). A National Sample Survey of 1960–61 yielded an average age of 18.45 years for urban women in Kerala (NSS Number 116, 1967:18). A survey of households in eight towns of Kerala, conducted in 1958–59, showed the daughters of the households as having an average age at marriage of about 18, their mothers about a year younger (Kurup and George 1969:38).

to 1956–1960).[8] A sharper rise, of 2.32 years, was shown for urban women, from 15.10 to 17.42 years. Men's average age at wedding increased less, by .79 year between the 1921 and 1961 Censuses, from 20.80 to 21.59 years. Male average age at effective marriage, according to National Sample Survey data, rose in the comparable period by 1.07 years for the rural men, from 20.83 to 21.90, and by .85 year for urban men, from 22.04 to 22.89 (Agarwala 1962a: 63–64; 1966a:52; NSS Number 154, 1970:4–6).

A few of the localized studies do not reflect such increases. An example of continuing low age at effective marriage is given in a study, done in 1948–50, of 1645 women in six villages near Delhi. Their median age at gauna was 14.4 years. The median figures for women who had married before 1930, from 1930 to 1950, and after 1950 were, respectively, 14.4, 14.4, and 14.5 years (Agarwala 1970: 72–75). But in a number of populous states and regions the average age at wedding has increased enough to demonstrate a relatively high age at effective marriage. The 1961 Census figures give average age at "formal marriage" as 17.46 years for the Punjab, 18.14 for Madras (Tamil Nadu), 18.54 for Assam, and 19.97 for Travancore in southern Kerala (Agarwala 1966a:32, 67; also see Jain 1967a:26–27).

Urban, educated women now begin their marriages at average ages close to the fertility-significant level. This is illustrated in a study of two middle-class *mohallas,* or neighborhoods, in Meerut

8. Agarwala has estimated (1966a:81–82) that the mean age of females at date of effective marriage has remained steady at 17 or 17.1 years through six Census decades up to 1961. These estimates, however, are based on some assumptions that do not accord with the evidence of the National Sample Survey data and of other studies (e.g., Karkal 1968).

Economic influences may not only affect age at marriage, as discussed next, but may also influence the working of grandmotherly shame. Concerning the exception noted in footnote 3, page 29, Dr. Jacobson points out that population density is still low in this area (Raisen district) and until the past few decades jungle land was freely available for clearing and cultivation. She writes "I would suspect that the pregnant grandmother ideology probably works to discourage those with sufficient children from having more, perhaps an important problem for landowners in areas of land scarcity." Lower status groups, she adds, have more births not because they are less ashamed of late pregnancies but because they need more offspring to guarantee the survival of "enough" children and the ideology therefore has a weaker influence on them.

city, northeast of Delhi. Most of the women under 40 there had a high school education or more. Among those who were 40 and older in 1966–67, the average age at marriage had been 15.3 and at gauna 16.5 years. But among those who were younger than 40, the average age at marriage was 17.4 and at gauna 18 years. By 1967 the wedding and the gauna rites were commonly celebrated within the same week. More than a third of the younger women had married at age 19 or older, but only 7.4% of their mothers had done so. The best age for a girl to marry, these people believe, is sixteen, but "Despite this firmly held belief, girls in these mohallas are increasingly being allowed to continue their education until seventeen or eighteen or even later, before they are married" (Vatuk 1969:165–168).

The villagers studied in the Khanna project show a similar disparity between an ideal, earlier age for a girl's marriage and the later, actual age of marriage. There also the average age of women at their nuptials has been rising steadily, increasing from 16.1 to 18 years between 1945–49 and 1959; the average age of men at nuptials has remained quite constant at just over 20 years. The authors of the study estimate that the women who began their effective marriage in 1959 would have 17% fewer children, because of their older average age at nuptials, than did their mothers and grandmothers (Wyon and Gordon 1971:154). When the data for age at nuptials in the period 1959–69 were gathered, it was found that the mean age of women at effective marriage had risen still higher. By 1969 it was 20.2 years; the 48 village daughters who were married out of the village in that year were, on the average, 20.6 years old, and the 56 brides who came into the village averaged 19.9 years at their nuptials.

The Khanna project did not accomplish its purpose of reducing fertility through wider acceptance of modern contraceptive methods, but Wyon and Gordon note that "The striking change in age of women at marriage is more important. The people themselves found reasons for delaying their daughter's marriage. If maintained, this could appreciably affect birth rates; it bodes well for the future practice of birth control" (*ibid.*:298–299).

Despite considerable exposure to family planning advice, these villagers remained largely unconvinced of the benefits to them personally of having fewer children (*ibid.*:297–298; Mamdani 1972). Yet without any outside urging to marry their daughters at a later age, they have done so and have done so despite their own ideas about the proper age for a girl's marriage. That ideal age is given by the Jat farmers as an average of 18, by the lower-ranking groups as 16 or less. The authors suggest that this difference in preferred age as well as the actual differences may be related to the opportunities and desire for the education of girls (Wyon and Gordon 1971:308). There has been a marked increase in girls' schooling among these villagers, especially in the higher-status groups, and this increase is apparently one of the reasons for the rising average age at marriage. But education is not the only factor that encourages fertility limitation. The women of the dominant Jats had lower fertility than did the women of the poor Chamars long before Jat girls had enough schooling to matter. Even in 1969 only some 40% of the Jat girls were being educated to the third grade or beyond, and only 4% of the Chamar girls, and yet the average age at marriage for all village girls had leaped from 16.1 to 20 in two decades (*ibid.*:251).

This delay in age at marriage, Mamdani concludes on the basis of his interviews in Manupur village, has been brought about largely because of economic reasons. The recent intensification of agriculture in the area has increased the work load of a farming family, not only in the fields but also in the home. Women's work, such as preparing and serving food, looking after animals, and collecting fuel, has become greater, partly because the men are busier in the fields and the women must now do more of the chores that the men formerly did. So the longer a girl remains unmarried, the longer her natal family has the benefit of her valuable work contribution. Furthermore, a grown, unmarried daughter can earn part of her dowry by weaving mats, sewing clothes, and spinning. Some of her products can be sold in the market town, and the rest can be set aside for her trousseau.

In the families of landless laborers as well, the age of the girls at effective marriage has risen sharply, in part at least because grown daughters can earn good wages, especially at periods of peak labor demand. Among the artisan and service groups of Manupur, particularly in the barber and tailor families, a similar rise in girls' age at marriage has occurred. The recently enhanced returns for girls' labor has apparently helped to quiet the parents' fears about having a nubile and yet unwed girl in the home. Why this dread, formerly so prevalent, has now receded is something that should be studied as a critical factor in the process. The fear has probably been allayed by such forces as the effect of increasing education and of a general shift in attitudes, as well as by the economic forces that Mamdani emphasizes. But he is right in observing that whatever decline there has been in the birth rate in Manupur has come about, not because of the Khanna project's efforts, but as a result of general technological and social change (Mamdani 1972:101–103, 117–118).

Not many village families have experienced the degree of technological change and of increased income that has occurred in the Khanna region. Nor have the villagers of the region as yet demonstrated any marked reduction in their fertility rates. They still share the traditional motivations for having children as well as the traditional motivations for controlling their fertility that we have noted in this chapter. But the lessons to be learned from the Khanna and other experimental projects indicate that economic, cultural, and social reasons together can persuade men and women to limit, directly or indirectly, the number of their children. Some clues concerning the effect of these forces may be derived from available studies of fertility rates in some principal categories of the Indian population.

THREE

◈

SOCIAL AND CULTURAL
DIFFERENTIALS

Social and Economic Status

PEOPLE of different social categories, as we have noted, tend to
have different fertility rates. The wealthier families in a locality,
who are usually (though not invariably) in the higher ranges of
the local caste hierarchy, tend to bear fewer children, on the
average, than their poorer and lower-ranking neighbors. The
wealthier families also generate most of the educated people.
Those who have a high school or college education have markedly
lower average fertility than do the less educated. Other social
factors that have been examined in relation to fertility are religion, urban residence, and joint family living. The data available
on all these factors are as yet fragmentary, and some of the studies
cited have major shortcomings. But it is nonetheless useful to
assess the available evidence for indications of the relative significance of these forces.

Women of lower and poorer groups tend to bear more children,
in part because more of their children die in infancy and so
these women have shorter lactation and anovulatory (nonovulat-
ing) periods before becoming fecund again, and in part because
they need more children to replace those they lose. So they continue to bear children at later ages. This difference is demonstrated in the Khanna study, where the Jat women who had been
married through their whole childbearing period had an average
of 7.0 live births, and the lower-ranking Chamar women averaged
8.2, some 15% more (Potter *et al.* 1965a:196; Wyon and Gordon
1971:140).[1]

1. One apparent exception to high fertility in the lowest caste category appears in a survey taken in Nagpur district. One of the groups of this

Several surveys have grouped residents into three ranked categories according to the status of their respective castes. The inverse relation of caste status and fertility is exemplified in a survey of 1413 Uttar Pradesh village couples. Women over 45 of the highest category averaged 7.6 live births, those of intermediate rank 8.2, and those of the lowest category 8.8 (Saxena 1965:141). In another survey of 2380 village couples in Banaras Tehsil, U.P., Hindu women of the highest category and married 30 years or more averaged 5.74 live births, those of intermediate rank 7.57, and those of the lowest category 6.93—fewer, it should be noted, than in the middle category (Rele 1963:184).

In the Mysore study, a regular relation does appear in the Bangalore city sample. There the women, 45 and over, of the highest category averaged 5.1 births, with 5.7 and 5.9 reported in the other two categories. But in the rural areas of Mysore, the higher-status women had an average of 4.9 as against 4.6 in each of the other two categories, and in the towns the comparable figures were 5.7, 4.0, and 5.0 (Mysore 1961:121).

A similar general tendency and similarly notable exceptions appear in the studies that take into account the narrower criterion of income in relation to fertility. Relevant data were collected in two rounds of the National Sample Survey. The reports show a regular decrease in fertility rates among classes with increasing income. In the round of 1960–61, the sample of 16,289 urban couples was classified into five categories, ranging from the lowest 20% in per capita monthly expeditures to the highest 20% in expenditures. Couples in the richest quintile had an average of 2.84 children born alive, and in the poorest 4.53. The comparable figures for children still living were 2.18 and 3.23 (NSS Number 116, 1967:32). Six categories of per capita monthly expenditure were noted in the sample of 39,469 rural respondents in the round of 1964–65. Those at the top level (Rs. 43 and above) had had an

---

"scheduled castes" category, the Mahar, is listed separately from the other Harijan castes of the bottom category. Mahar women show one of the lowest mean fertility figures among thirteen groups, though the other scheduled castes had the highest mean fertility of all (Driver 1963:90). But the Mahars are noted in the region as being better organized, more militant, and probably better off than the other groups ranked in the lowest category.

annual birth rate per thousand persons of 32.30; those in the lowest (Rs. 0–11) bracket, 44.28. Among 23,720 urban respondents, the comparable figures were 25.35 and 43.05 (NSS Number 186, 1970:5).

Some of the more localized surveys, however, do not reflect such regular gradations, and several report that people in the highest income categories also have high fertility (see Mysore 1961:124; Agarwala 1966a:99–101). A possible reason for this has been suggested for prospering rural families. "For this group, the initial effect of increased incomes is likely to be an improvement in health and nutritional levels which could significantly increase fecundity and live fertility rates, as well as the number of persons completing their fertile period" (Ridker 1969a:283; also see Hawthorn 1970:71–73). This suggestion is a likely explanation but has yet to be tested with a suitable range of data. It may well indicate the *first* part of a general process whereby newly prospering families have more births for a time because their improved standard of nutrition and health brings about fewer miscarriages, less sterility, and fewer deaths among women before they have completed their reproductive span. The other part of the process begins when such prospering families adopt patterns of higher caste and class status. These standards, as we shall discuss later, require greater sex discipline and result in lower fertility.

Fertility Differentials: Religion

Religious affiliation may have some bearing on fertility rates, though the operative forces seem to be more economic and educational than directly religious. Muslims showed higher fertility rates than did Hindus in the census reports for undivided India (Davis 1951:80, 191–194, 199). Most of the surveys done since 1947 in what are now India and Bangladesh corroborate the earlier differentials (Mysore 1961:119; Rele 1963:185, 198; Agarwala 1966a:97–98; K. Dandekar 1967:59; El-Badry 1967:634; Srinivasan 1967:56; Stoeckel and Choudhury 1969a:190). But a few nationwide surveys and local studies give different results. In the National Sample Surveys taken in 1953–54 and 1960–61, Muslims do show decidedly higher fertility rates than others, by some 14% and even a bit more in some categories. But in the round of 1963–64, rural Muslims produced slightly lower fertility rates (and slightly lower mortality rates also) than did rural Hindus. The urban sample in 1963–64 recorded very similar fertility rates for Hindus and Muslims, as did the general sample in the round of 1964–65 (NSS Number 54, 1962:34–35; Number 116, 1967:26; Number 175, 1970:5; Number 177, 1970:13).

In two small-scale studies of West Bengal villagers, Muslims showed lower fertility rates than did most of their Hindu neighbors (Nag 1962:48–62; Rao and Mathen 1970:20). The analysis made by Moni Nag, using data collected in 1960 by Dr. Uma Guha in a cluster of three West Bengal villages, distinguished fertility performance among Muslims of two classes, the landowning, better-educated Sheikh and the quite poor, relatively uneducated "non-Sheikh." While the whole Muslim sample yielded a lower fertility rate than did the Hindu, the Sheikh Muslims had higher fertility than their poorer co-religionists. Nag suspects (p. 61) that the prevalence of veneral disease among the non-Sheikhs may reduce their natality through sterility and miscarriages.

Muslims in most of the world commonly do generate high fertility, often higher than that of their non-Muslim neighbors (Kirk 1966). In India some part of this was because of the greater number of remarried widows among them, but this accounted for only about a third of the differential before 1941 (Davis 1951:81); in recent decades, as we have noted, it has been of even less significance. Probably of some significance were the greater values that Hindus place on abstinence and religious celibacy, the longer visits of young Hindu wives to their parents' home, the more numerous sacred Hindu occasions that require sexual abstinence (Mysore 1961:120; Nag 1965; 1972:236–237; Chaudhury 1971).

Where modern contraceptive devices have been made available, Muslims seem less likely to use them than do Hindus. Thus among villagers surveyed near Comilla, now Bangladesh, more Hindu couples (11.5%) had "ever practiced family planning" than had Muslim couples (6.3%); the Hindus "consistently practicing" were 10.4%; Muslims 3.8% (Stoeckel and Choudhury

1969b:34). Similar findings emerge from studies done in India (see K. Dandekar 1967:59; Krishnakumar 1971:151). Although some Muslims give religious reasons for not controlling fertility, a significant cause of their higher fertility is economic and educational. A greater proportion of Indian Muslims than of caste Hindus are at the poorer and less educated levels of society, levels at which people of all religions have higher fertility (see Weiner 1970:11–12; Aitken and Stoeckel 1971).

Birth rates for four religious groups—Christians, Hindus, Muslims, and Sikhs—were calculated from the 1963–64 round of the National Sample Survey (Number 175, 1970:5). In both rural and urban samples, Christians showed the lowest birth rates, followed by Sikhs. For rural Christians the average annual births per thousand persons was 30.58, for rural Hindus 38.07. Urban Christians were still lower, 29.97 as against 31.61 for urban Hindus. In the Mysore study, the Christians of Bangalore city, who are relatively well educated, had markedly lower fertility than did people of other religions in this city (Mysore 1961:119). But other Christians, without educational advantages, showed higher fertility in some surveys than did Hindus (*ibid.*:119; Srinivasan 1967:56; NSS Number 116, 1967:26). The Parsis of Bombay, Zoroastrians in religion and a community that has one of the highest levels of education and income in India, appear in El-Badry's study to have the lowest fertility rate among the religious groups of Bombay (1967:633; see also Ketayun Gould 1972b). The relation between religion and fertility seems to have as much to do with levels of income and education among the followers of a religion as it does with any specific precepts of that religion.

Fertility Differentials: Urban Residence and Joint Family

The population of towns and cities through most of the world show lower average birth rates than do rural populations. This is so in India also, though the relation is not always consistent nor has it been, in past decades, very significant demographically. The Census of India figures do show that, in general, urban residents have lower birth rates than do rural people, but the Census definition of an urban locality as any place with over 5000 population is so broad as to obscure important variation (Chandra Sekhar

1971:3; Gould 1972b). Although additional kinds of urban places were distinguished by the Census of 1961 and 1971,[2] the basic threshold figure of 5000 was retained. Studies of the Census returns and survey data indicate that the urban-rural differential was not, at least until 1961, a significant factor in India's population growth, partly because of the small proportion of urban people in the nation and partly because of the narrowness of the difference in fertility rates (Davis 1951:70–71; Mathen 1962:289; Driver 1963:7–8, 85–87; Paulus 1966:82, 99).

National Sample Surveys also show lower crude birth rates for the urban than for the rural samples (NSS Number 175, 1970:5; Number 177, 1970:8). But if a more precise index of fertility is derived, urban couples are seen to have as high fertility as have rural, or even a bit higher. Thus the births per thousand people are reported as 34.28 for the urban sample and 37.32 for the rural sample in the round of 1964–65 (NSS Number 186, 1970:5). When the preponderance of males in urban areas is factored out by calculating the rates of marital fertility (birth per thousand currently married females aged 15–44), the fertility rate for the urban sample is a bit higher than that for the rural sample, 216.52 to 211.34 (ibid.:8). Within the urban and rural samples, this rate was calculated according to income categories (monthly per capita expenditure). The urban sample shows a higher marital fertility rate in four of the six categories; at the poorest level, the urban rate is 327.40 as against 287.34 in the rural sample. Urban women had markedly lower fertility only in the wealthiest class (Rs. 43 and above), with a rate of 162.67 as compared with 171.37 for rural women of this bracket of per capita monthly expenditure.

Both rural and urban people apparently respond to better health and nutritional conditions with an initial rise in fertility rates. This rise may well be the reason that couples married after 1941 had significantly higher fertility, as reported from the NSS round of 1963–64, than couples married before 1941.[3] The in-

2. The 1971 Census stipulated that to be listed as urban, a habitation area had to have a minimum of 75% of working males in non-agricultural occupations and a minimum of 400 people per square kilometer.

3. One great health improvement has been in subduing the incidence and effects of malaria. This disease used to be a prime cause of the many miscarriages and spontaneous abortions (Learmonth 1958:10; Newman 1965).

crease was greater for urban than for rural couples, but the report allows that "this may be due to lower widowhood rate and less recall bias of the urban couples" (NSS Number 175, 1970:11). The subsequent shift by prospering people to patterns of lower fertility is made more quickly in a large city and more slowly in middle-sized towns, according to the evidence of the Mysore study. The marital fertility rate in the sample from Bangalore city (then over 779,000 in population) was 199, considerably lower than the 237 figure from the sample of rural plains people. The marital fertility rate of the sample from towns of 10,000 to 25,000 population was 251, higher than either. And women of the middle and wealthier families (on a simple three-part scale) in these towns produced higher birth rates than did townswomen of the poorest category, quite opposite to the Bangalore results, in which wealthier, better-educated women had fewer births than did women of lower categories (Mysore 1961:83–85).

Infant mortality is one demographic aspect in which the urban rates are consistently lower than the rural. Infant and child mortality is so high through most of India that parents commonly feel, as we have previously noted, they must have many babies in order to make sure of having a few grown children. With better control of epidemic disease in recent decades, child mortality in ages one to five is not as high as it used to be (see Wyon and Gordon 1971:188, 205). But the infant mortality rates, the ratio of deaths of infants less than a year in age to live births, continues to be very high among rural people. Infant deaths are much lower among urban people, though still drastically severe in comparison to the rates in wealthier societies. Thus the annual infant mortality rates in the urban samples of three NSS surveys are 84.67, 80, 79.39; the comparable figures for rural samples are 116.85, 114, 127.29 (NSS Number 175, 1970:7; Number 177, 1970:8; Number 186, 1970:9).

The infant mortality rate, too, varies by level of income and education. In the Mysore study, rural landless laborers suffered an infant mortality rate that was half again as much as the average for all rural classes. In the samples from Mysore towns and from Bangalore city the poorest people also lost a far greater proportion of their infants than did those who were better off (Mysore 1961:81). A particularly striking difference is given in the relatively reliable registrations of infant mortality in Bombay city. The rates were calculated by religion, with Hindus divided into "scheduled castes" and "other castes." In 1946–47, Muslims, "other caste" Hindus, and Indian Christians showed infant mortality rates of 189, 185, and 179 respectively. But the poorest "scheduled castes" recorded 308 as compared with a rate of 72 for the better educated, higher-income Parsis (Chandrasekhar 1972: 147).

It seems likely that both the higher and the lower infant mortality rates have intensifier effects on fertility rates. That is, those couples who follow a high fertility pattern tend to produce even more births if many of their infants die, because a mother then has a shorter infertile period following termination of pregnancy. S. Chandrasekhar has summarized the evidence that the higher the birth rate, the higher the infant mortality rate (1972:260–261). The obverse is also true: the higher the infant mortality, the more offspring are produced. But for couples who follow patterns of lower fertility, whether through traditional controls or modern ones, low infant mortality helps assure them that their children have a good chance of surviving and so they need not try for additional births as insurance. In the Khanna study, the number of children borne by couples of both the wealthier Jat farmers and the poorer Chamar leather workers was affected by the number of children each couple had lost. "Among wives of the farmer caste, particularly, survival of most of their children born early during the process of family building was associated with relatively few subsequent births" (Wyon and Gordon 1971:197–198, 205). Many more Jat couples than Chamar received the assurance of having their children survive, and thus many more limited their fertility by traditional methods. In cities, the better-off, better-educated couples gain such assurance readily and apparently shift to lower fertility rates more quickly than their counterparts in towns and villages.

That city couples in other parts of the world produce fewer children on the average than do rural couples has sometimes been attributed to a shift in cities from joint families to small, nuclear families. In these small families, the explanation continues, many children become a liability rather than an asset, and so couples limit the number they have (see Hall 1972:212–213). A key element in this explanation is the presumably greater encouragement to high fertility in joint families. But a review of the worldwide evidence of this factor concludes, with emphasis, "Clearly the widespread conviction that extended family structure is (statistically) associated with—let alone a *cause* of—high fertility is not yet empirically warranted" (Burch and Gendell 1971:102).

In India that association seems, if anything, to be reversed. Women living in joint families apparently have fewer children on the average than those in nuclear families. That finding has been reported from studies of rural people in Puri district of Orissa, in Delhi state, in West Bengal, and elsewhere in India and in Bangladesh (Bebarta 1961:34–35; 1966:33; Pakrasi and Malaker 1967:455; Datta 1961:80; Nag 1965; Stoeckel and Choudhury 1969a:194; Burch and Gendell 1971:91). Lower fertility among city women living in joint families has been reported in studies from Bombay, Lucknow, Karachi, and Calcutta (Straus and Winkelman 1969:66–68; Husain 1970a:46–47; Hashmi 1965:102; Datta 1961:81; Pakrasi and Malaker 1967:457). It has been suggested that because couples living in joint families have less privacy they are likely to have less frequent intercourse and therefore fewer children (Hashmi 1965:103; Nag 1965:136; Gould 1972a:250). But the relation between privacy and coital frequency has not been empirically established nor has any such reduction in frequency been shown to result in lowered fertility.

What is probably more cogent is the typical family cycle: a newly married couple lives with the husband's parents and brothers until eventually the married brothers separate into nuclear families, each of which again becomes a joint family when the sons bring in their brides. Among lower-ranking, poorer people, the joint family stage is likely to be short, and so poorer groups show a higher proportion of nuclear families than do the wealthier classes (Mandelbaum 1970:125–130). Since poor, uneducated people have more births on the average than do the more affluent, the higher fertility reported for nuclear families may come out of greater poverty rather than lesser privacy, and out of lack of education rather than more coital frequency. Those whose life circumstances are favorable to joint family living are likely to maintain stricter family discipline, especially of the mother-in-law over her daughters-in-law (Nag 1972:237). The mother-in-law in a joint family may see to it that her daughters-in-law observe the taboos which bring about traditionally proper birth spacings and that she herself manages to stop having children when her daughters-in-law begin.

In any event, urbanization in India has not so far brought about any general lowering of fertility in the way it has in Japan or Europe (Morrison 1961; Myrdal 1968:1441). One clear reason is that the towns and cities still hold large numbers of the very poor and uneducated, and although the wealthier, better-educated urban families do curtail their fertility, the poor have not had the means or motivation to do so.

Fertility Differentials: Education

Of the modern social factors that influence fertility, the education of girls is particularly relevant to family-planning policies because increased public investment in it should bring about reduced fertility relatively quickly and with continuing effect. The relevant surveys show that women who have attended high school have significantly fewer children, on the average, than those with less education. The general tendency is for fertility rates to go down as the number of years in school goes up, a principal exception being that women with only a little schooling, who are just barely literate, average more children than do illiterate women. Perhaps this is a reflection of the trend we have noted before, that those poor families whose members begin to attain better nutrition and health resources increase their fertility for a time before taking on the higher-status behavior patterns that lower fertility (see Datta 1961:78; Hawthorn 1970:76).

In the NSS round of 1960–61, 16,285 urban women aged 47 and older were interviewed, and their responses were grouped according to six educational classes, from illiterate to "college and above." The average number of children born alive to women who had had only primary schooling was 6.57; for those with a middle-school education it was 5.04; and for matriculates (high school graduates) it was 4.58. The sharpest decrease was between the latter and the 2.01 average for those who had attended college (NSS Number 116, 1967:22).

The report of the 1961–62 round includes a rural sample (of 32,453 women) as well as an urban sample (22,301), though neither is stratified by age (NSS Number 154, 1970:12). Both show a decrease in average number of children born alive with an increase in women's educational class above the primary level. The rural women show the largest decrease between the primary (2.62) and the middle-school level (2.31). The largest decline in the urban sample comes one level higher, between the middle school (2.60) and the secondary level (2.06).

In the Mysore study, four categories of women's education were listed, but only in Bangalore city were there sufficient numbers for statistical analysis of respondents in all four categories (Mysore 1961:122, 128). Not much difference in fertility appeared among the city women in the categories up to "high school or university." There was a sharp decline there: the average number of children born alive (for ever-married women aged 45 and over) was 5.5 in the middle-school category and 3.9 for women of high school and university education. In the town sample the usual relation was reversed (as it was in the income classification): women over 45 with a middle-school education reported a higher average number, 7.0, than did women with primary schooling, 6.8. The rural sample in this study yielded comparable data only on illiterate women (4.7) and those with some primary school education (6.6).

Driver's survey in Nagpur district set up three classes of women's education (in a sample of 2314): none, primary school, above primary school. Again there was a sharp decline in the highest category; the weighted mean of children born alive among women of all ages was 4.7 for those in the primary school category, 3.8 for those with education above the primary level (Driver 1963:101).

Finally, the survey taken of 4420 households in Lucknow city in 1966–67 reports general fertility rates by class of education (Husain 1970a:49, 120; 1970b). All the women in a household were for some unstated reason put in the educational class of the female member with the highest education. The tabulations show a steady decline in general fertility rate (per thousand) with increasing education, even from illiterate (163.89) to the next category "below primary" (145.16), and through primary (102.04), secondary (96.20), and higher (63.38). This survey also calculated fertility rates by level of husband's education. The results are similar but with some lag in fertility decline, since a man and his family usually require that his wife have an education congruent with his own but a notch or two less. The available data do not as yet allow for calibrated conclusions as to how many fewer children are produced by how much more education for girls. It is clear that only a year or two of schooling results in little or no reduction in fertility but that a high school education regularly has significant effect.

Many parents now want to educate their girls, partly as a wise investment toward obtaining a worthy husband for a beloved daughter. To be sure, there are also many who would agree with the prevailing opinion in one Madhya Pradesh village, as Dr. Doranne Jacobson reported it, that schooling for girls is a complete waste, that educated girls are prone to all kinds of misfortune—"barrenness, shrewishness, or widowhood" (1970:107–108). But the tide of opinion among economically rising villagers and even more among prospering townspeople is in quite the other direction.

A main avenue for social rise nowadays, even for villagers, is through modern education for one's sons. It is also essential, now as before, to arrange prestigious marriages for daughters if a family is to achieve and maintain higher status within its group. A bridegroom who has had a good education is prized, and such a young man commonly requires that his bride also be educated. Those families who have the will to rise in social status within their communities (and very many do in India as elsewhere) and have the wherewithal to make the attempt (and more have it now than formerly) are inclined to send their daughters to school and keep them there for longer than was thought necessary or proper in earlier generations.

Keeping a girl in her natal family through high school, and even more so through college, has meant that her parents had to gird themselves against what used to be the discomfort and immanent shame of having a pubescent, unmarried girl in the house, exposed to temptations and so a potential millstone on the family's honor. But in recent times an unbetrothed girl who is in high school or college has come to be less vulnerable to rumor and castigation. Her family has been better able to withstand the still worrisome years between her menarche and her marriage, in order that they may eventually be able to arrange a match for her that will help lift her heart and their status.

Why, then, does keeping a girl in school tend in later years to reduce her total fertility as a married woman? In some small part the schooling is a direct cause in that girls are not usually married while they are still attending high school or college. Hence educated girls tend to be married at a later average age, some of them late enough to help reduce the total number of children they eventually bear (see Mysore 1961:98–99, 108; Driver 1963: 71; NSS Number 154, 1970:4; Husain 1970a:29–30; 1970b:134–136). More importantly, an educated couple usually shares a life style in which there is less reason to have many children and more reason to have fewer. Educated people curtailed their fertility before family planning advice was widespread and before there was significant use of modern contraceptive measures. We do not yet have detailed studies to tell just how they absorbed ideas about family limitation, but some firm impressions on this score can be gained from our general anthropological and sociological knowledge.

An educated woman is usually less closely confined, physically and psychologically, within her husband's family and its narrow familial concerns than is the woman who is brought into their home as an uneducated girl shortly after her menarche. Village elders commonly tell you, and they are probably right, that a young wife who has been to high school or college is not as duly submissive to her mother-in-law as is a less educated daughter-in-law, nor will she brook the kind of social restraints that the strict tradition requires. She is more likely to feel that she can do something about certain conditions of her life, including the condition of pregnancies in close succession or conceiving during her later reproductive years. Her schooling has commonly disclosed to her more leeway in her *karma,* more alternatives in her *dharma,* than an uneducated woman can know. Her horizons of information are wider, if only from being able to read a newspaper; her network of communication is likely to be broader, if only to school friends beyond the confines of household and kin. These differences are not, of course, direct results of her having studied algebra or learned to read another language, but they are potent consequences that help her shape her life and are likely to induce her to limit her fertility. Both educated and uneducated brides still know well that they have to prove themselves by bearing children, but the educated wife is not as likely to want to keep proving herself through obstetrical channels throughout the whole reproductive span of her life.

Moreover, the fact of her education as a girl is an index to the likelihood that she will marry into a family with enough resources to afford some medical care for her children and that she can keep more of them alive through the perilous early years. She is likely to be a bit more secure about being cared for in her old age, to feel less dreadfully precarious about the survival of her sons. Both she and her husband will be better able to tap varied resources in their times of need than will an uneducated, poor couple, and so they will feel less totally dependent for safety on a large number of children. A husband who has had a high school or college education may or may not have gained much substantively from it, but he has usually learned to value the kind of self-discipline and future-planning that accords with fertility control. And an educated man is less likely to insist on a maximum number of sons to help him in the toil of the field and the struggle of the feud, especially if he toils elsewhere than in the village fields and engages in struggles other than those of village feuds.

Girls who are now in high school or college are likely, when they are married women in their thirties, to hold these motiva-

tions for smaller families more strongly and to act on them more
effectively than did educated women of the older generation.
Girls' education is far more common than it was, though the
general level is still low. An educated woman will no longer have
to hold out alone against pressures to keep on bearing children;
her inclinations may well be supported and reinforced by educated kinfolk and friends.

In some groups, the increase in girls' education has been
very great. In a sample of eighteen households in one Punjab village, Kamla Nath reports, all the women over 35 were illiterate,
but all the girls between 6 and 14 were attending school (1965:
815). In two middle-class sections (mohallas) of Meerut city,
Sylvia Vatuk writes, the older women (40 and over) averaged 2.8
years of education; virtually all their unmarried daughters to age
16 were still in school (1969:73–77). Dr. Vatuk's study focuses on
kinship and tells how a young wife's kinship relations have
changed among these middle-class city people. The young woman
is now much less wholly incorporated into and encapsulated by
her husband's family; she is more her husband's reliant wife and
not so constantly her mother-in-law's daughter-in-law. Her relations with neighbors of the mohalla tend to be more like those
traditionally proper in a woman's natal village, where she feels
freer as a daughter, rather than like those traditional in the
husband's village, where she must comport herself as a restricted,
restrained daughter-in-law (1969:126, 230, 262–263). A young wife
in the city milieu will probably be inclined to let her husband
know of her feelings about numerous births and is less likely to
remain silent while nature takes her course. One reason given in
these mohallas for educating a girl is to provide her with the
ability to take care of herself and her children should her husband
die. Traditionally a widow is cared for by her affines, her husband's kin. But among these middle-class city families, a widow is
expected to prefer to take care of herself. Actually very few of the
educated women among them have to support themselves or take
employment outside the home (Vatuk 1969:140–141).[4]

4. Women's employment, in itself, is not in India the significant force in
lowering fertility that it has been in some more industrialized societies. Edu-

Not readily measurable but also not least among the factors that persuade educated men and women to control their fertility is the power of the ideas to which they are exposed. For some in the older generation, Gandhi's message of limitation through abstinence had effect. Younger men and women, those who have attended high school since the start of the government's family planning campaign, know that family planning is feasible and that official authority says that it is highly desirable (see Kale 1969:28). And indeed the proportion of those who use modern contraceptive devices rises steadily with increasing education (see Sen and Sen 1967a:20; NSS Number 154, 1970:91; Husain 1970a:100–101; Kripalani et al. 1971). With the new emphasis given to family planning in schools and in the mass media, the effect of girls' education on their fertility as women may well be intensified.

In sum, among the several social factors whose influence on fertility we have considered, joint family living appears to be quite irrelevant. Religion may be of some significance, but more as a background variable than as a direct influence. Different groups of Indian Christians, for example, have different fertility rates according to their levels of income and education. Although Muslim aggregate fertility rates have been higher than those of the other major religions, some of the recent surveys indicate that the difference is diminishing or, in some localities, has disappeared. As for the Parsis, certainly their Zoroastrian religion does not explain their low average fertility, though it may have been a factor in encouraging their economic and educational achievements.

The growth of India's cities seems to have had little dampening effect as yet on the growth of the nation's population. The evidence now available points to higher income and education as the critical factors in lowering average fertility in cities and towns as

cated women who are employed do have fewer children but more as a consequence of their education than of their employment. Uneducated women who must work to help keep their families afloat do not have significantly fewer children, on the average, than they would if they were not working (Driver 1963:94; Minkler 1970; Dhillon 1970).

well as in villages. Because educational opportunities are generally greater in urban areas, because health facilities are somewhat more available, and because governmental urgings can be more effectively communicated, it seems probable that more urban than village people will shift to patterns of lower fertility and will make the shift more rapidly.

In the traditional mode, that shift was characteristically made by families of middle or lower status who were ambitious and were prospering. They typically sought to lift their caste rank by emulating the ritual prerogatives and life style of their neighbors of the higher, "twice-born" categories of castes. High caste rank was not supposed to rest on anything other than innate ritual purity, but in actual practice there was unceasing competition to attain and maintain high caste status. A group could not succeed in adopting new and higher customs unless it had the necessary wealth and was united in strength of will and arms (Mandelbaum 1970:425–520). The prestigious styles of life required—among other things, but importantly among them—that the behavior of women be more strictly controlled and that discipline in sex relations become more stringent. Taking on a loftier way of life also meant becoming more self-controlled for purposes of proper birth spacing and, particularly, in avoiding the shame of becoming a pregnant grandmother—or the husband of one.[5]

Competition for status is still a central feature of village life, but the symbols of high status and the terms of the competition have somewhat altered. There are village men who fought strenuously for the right to wear the sacred thread, emblem of the "twice-born," who find their sons and grandsons uninterested in that ancient privilege, although they are most interested in acquiring contemporary insignia of high status. Modern education has become a requirement for the most desired kinds of livelihood, and so ambitious families who can afford the cost are generally eager to educate their sons. As we have seen, this step re-

5. This process has occurred in other parts of the world. One worldwide survey concludes that "a fertility decline in a country typically begins with women trying to end reproduction earlier, attempts to space children follow later" (Presser 1970:32).

quires keeping their daughters in school also, and possibly delaying their marriages long enough to lower fertility rates. Couples of this better-educated generation may not be quite so concerned as were their parents about observing the traditional postpartum periods of abstinence or about grandmotherly shame, but they are likely to have acquired other motivations to limit their fertility. Yet the traditional motives and methods for limiting family size are still important, and we turn now to them.

FOUR

TRADITIONAL METHODS OF
LIMITING FERTILITY

How did Indian women and men manage to limit the number of their children? We have seen that a good many succeeded in doing so long before there was an official Family Planning Programme, before pills for the purpose were developed, before vasectomy and tubectomy were significant possibilities, and when the only mechanical means used was the condom and that was used effectively by exceedingly few. The methods they did, and do, use effectively include a good deal of abstinence, some practice of coitus interruptus, and a considerable number of induced abortions.

Some sexual abstinence for a man is considered to be good for him. As Moni Nag has put it, "There is a widespread belief among Hindus that semen is a great source of strength for men and so men are very much concerned about loss of their strength through coitus" (1972:235). Semen is considered to be life-maintaining as well as life-generating, and, in the popular belief, a man has only a small, limited store of it, each drop formed at the cost of forty (or in some versions, one hundred times one hundred) drops of his blood. So the loss of semen is believed to dilute a man's energies, thicken his wits, and if "excessive" may drain away his life (see Gould 1969b:1517; Wyon and Gordon 1971: 86; Poffenberger and Poffenberger 1973:45). Tuberculosis, the principal cause of death among young adults, is often ascribed to sexual overindulgence. And mothers of infants should have as few sex acts as possible; in popular belief a nursing infant may be imperiled if the mother has intercourse because her breast milk may thereby become spoiled (Pathare 1966:52; C. E. Taylor 1968:157; Gould 1969a:1889–1890; Poffenberger and Poffenberger 1973:28).

A man who is celibate is believed to conserve his physical strength, to enhance his spiritual stamina, and to give himself a start toward supernal attainments. This concept is rooted in Hindu scripture and was most vigorously publicized in modern times by Gandhi. Through much of his writing and teaching, Gandhi emphasized the moral elevation that a man can attain through celibacy and the profound moral depletion attendant upon lustful indulgence. He wrote on the need for birth control —but only through sexual abstinence (see Gandhi 1947; 1962). Not all in India agreed with him; most Muslims, among others, felt that Gandhi's ideas on this subject were divergent from their own religious tradition. Yet a good many Indian Muslims, like their countrymen of other faiths, also are concerned about excessive loss of semen (see Carstairs 1957:85; Nag 1972:236).

Lately a few of Gandhi's followers have begun to question his rigorous position on celibacy and birth control (see Narayan 1968; B. L. Atreya, quoted in R. W. Taylor 1969:19–20). Some scholars, in reexamining the scriptural sources, have cited such dicta as the one from Manu that a man is as good as celibate if he visits his wife only on two nights in a month (Tripathi 1969:73). These discussions reach only a few and, indeed, great as was Gandhi's influence in some matters, there is no indication that his strong urgings to the masses that they practice birth control through abstinence had much mass effect. What does seem to affect fertility is men's favorable inclination toward some periods of abstinence for the sake of their physical health and spiritual vigor.

One result of this disposition is a relatively low average frequency of intercourse by married couples, at least as compared with the frequencies recorded by Kinsey and his associates for couples in the United States (Wyon and Gordon 1971:155; Nag 1972:235). From her interviews in an Uttar Pradesh village, Ketayun Gould has identified (1969a:1889) three phases of a couple's sexual relations. The first lasts from the nuptial rites until a healthy child is born and survives infancy. The husband's parents, as was noted above, are eager for a grandchild and give the young couple as much privacy as possible at night, a separate room if available. The couple has sexual relations frequently, even skimping or ignoring periods of ritual taboo. The next phase occurs between the birth of the couple's first child and the immanence of their first grandchild. The frequency of intercourse is very much reduced, partly from lessened opportunity, party from more faithful observance of various taboo periods. There is less opportunity because even after the period of postpartum abstinence (commonly a year in this village), a husband and wife there do not usually sleep in the same room.

Among many North Indian groups, men and women occupy separate social and physical space; a man enters the women's quarters only for a specific purpose and limited stay. Families that can afford it have a separate shelter where the men sleep and spend their leisure time. In villages of Etawah district, U. P., Raghuraj Gupta writes that the men "visit their wives late at night and soon return to the male quarters, unseen and undetected," for a man becomes a subject of ridicule and gossip if it is said that he daily sleeps with his wife. But, Gupta adds, the poor in these villages who have only a one-room hut "cannot afford this luxury of abstinence" (1965:5). The poor are also less likely to be as stringent about observing taboo periods or honoring as many such periods as do wealthier folk.

In the third stage of marital sexual relations, Dr. Gould observes, the shame of a woman's becoming pregnant (and so giving evidence of continued sexual activity) while her own child is having children is a dominant concern. During this phase, "most couples report either extremely infrequent sexual relations or none" (Gould 1969a:1890). From her interviews with women in this village, Dr. Gould (1972a) provides a table of average frequency of coitus per normal (nontaboo) week for married women, sorted into seven age groups. The sharpest decline in frequency is from ages 25–29 (2.0) to ages 30–34 (0.8), with a slight rise for ages 35–39 (1.0).

Similar curtailment of frequency has been reported by married women in their thirties elsewhere in India. In three West Bengal villages, the average weekly frequencies for 172 Hindu women were reported as 1.8 at ages 25–29, 1.1 at ages 30–34, and 0.7 at ages 35–39 (Nag 1972:235). The reports of 60 women from a well-to-do Calcutta suburb (as recast from the original form of tabulation) give weekly average frequencies of 2.0 at ages 25–29, 1.0 at ages 30–34, and 0.9 at ages 35–39 (Sengupta 1965:58). By comparison, the mean weekly frequency for American white women aged 31–35 in the Kinsey sample is 2.3, while that for Indian women aged 30–34 is 1.1 for Bengali Hindus, 0.8 for an Uttar Pradesh village, and 1.0 for a Calcutta suburb. The frequencies for Muslims in the West Bengal sample are higher—1.8 for the Sheikh women aged 30–34 and 2.1 for non-Sheikhs—but for them also the greatest decline in frequency comes after ages 25–29 and during the years 30–34 (Nag 1972:235).

The research workers on the Khanna project separately interviewed husbands and wives of 1094 couples about their frequency of intercourse. Many were averse to answering the question; among those who did answer, the wives tended to report less frequency than did their husbands. These figures also show a marked reduction in frequency during a woman's thirties. For married woman aged 15–24, 45% reported a frequency of at least once a week, and 25% at least once a month but not each week. By ages 35–39, only 11% reported the higher frequency and 47% the lower. The authors conclude that "From these limited data, a probable understatement of fact, coitus is sufficiently infrequent in the community after the wife reaches approximately age 35 that it affects considerably the chance of conception. Toward the end of childbearing life, intervals between coitus were sufficiently long to consider abstinence as deliberately practiced for birth control" (Wyon and Gordon 1971:155).[1]

At just what level a declining average frequency of coitus begins to reduce average fertility is not now known because the critical factor is not mean frequency per week or month but

1. These authors also note that in the Khanna region the frequency of intercourse varies with the seasons, since couples sleep together more often in the winter for warmth (Wyon and Gordon 1971:85). Several studies of the monthly rate of conception in various parts of India conclude that the rate of conception is much higher in the colder months than in the hot months. In the cities climate alone tends to be a major influence, but among rural people the effect of the climate is mediated by the work demands of the agricultural calendar and by the plenitude available after the harvest (Planalp 1971:108–116; Stoeckel and Choudhury 1971).

whether a woman has sexual relations during the fertile 48 hours
or less of her menstrual cycle. For this reason, D. I. Pool questions the importance of the frequency factor, at least on the so-
cietal level (1972:253). Indian couples who want to postpone or
avoid another pregnancy probably rely on periods of abstinence
rather than on less frequent intercourse during "normal" weeks.

Periods of Abstinence

A main reason for long abstention, as we have seen, is lactation.
Those women who nurse their children for a year or more and
whose husbands honor the taboo on intercourse during the lactation period can space their pregnancies and so reduce their total
fertility. Another reason for abstinence is the illness of either
partner. Abstention during illness is practiced in all groups of a
village near Meerut (called Bunkipur by the author), partly
lest the sick person become further weakened by having intercourse and partly to avoid the spread of a contagious disease
through intimate contact. Given the relatively high rate of disease
in this village, Marshall notes, these prohibitions probably have
an important effect on the frequency of intercourse (1972a:149–
150). In the Khanna region, the sickness of any family member is
a reason for abstinence (Wyon and Gordon 1971:85).

There is one kind of abstinence, however, that paradoxically
may result in higher rather than lower fertility. It is popularly
believed that a woman's most fertile period comes in the days
immediately following the cessation of menstruation and that the
rest of the menstrual cycle is "safer." Sexual relations are forbidden during menstruation and almost all couples rigorously observe this taboo. But in a number of groups a postmenstrual taboo
period is also favored. In a sample of women from Mysore villages, 66% reported abstinence for at least 8 days after onset, as
did 40% of the women in a sample from a middle-class part of
Delhi. Some women reported up to 15 days of abstinence after
onset. As C. Chandrasekaran points out, with such abstinence periods "the timing of coitus appears to coincide with the days of
the woman's ovulation" (1952:78). This misapprehension apart,

observance of the biologically signaled periods of abstinence has helped reduce fertility rates.

A couple typically observes some abstention during religious occasions, but the number of such periods varies among individuals and groups at different stages of a couple's married life. Young couples typically refrain much less often than do older couples who have several healthy sons. The number of ritually tabooed days listed by respondents from Mysore villages came to a median of 24 in a year, but the range of responses was from 2 to 120. In a Delhi neighborhood, the median was 19, the range 1 to 79. (*ibid.:*78). For Bengal villages the number of tabooed days has been variously estimated at 70 and at nearly 100 (Nag 1965:136; 1972:236–237; Mathen 1962:42), but these figures in themselves do not reflect the effective realities. A younger, sonless couple will abstain only on the two or three most sacred periods of the year; a less anxious pair will probably abstain during any period of fasting, since abstention from food can be taken to mean abstention from sex also. Poorer, lower-ranking people, as we have noted, tend to observe fewer fast days (see Saxena 1965:141). Most of them have to work daily to get their daily food and do not have enough surplus to be able to afford the costs of ritual or the loss of a day's wage. In the village near Meerut, for example, the low-ranking Chamar women kept only three fast days a year, but some of the wealthier Thakur women observed forty or more fast days each year (Marshall 1972a:149).

A matron who has several sons, secure family income, respectable caste rank, and a cooperative husband can turn up a good many occasions that are ritually forbidden for sexual relations. There are two or three inauspicious day of the week, two or more inauspicious phases of the lunar months, many local and regional ceremonial periods. To these she can add familial occasions, such as the death anniversary of a parent or period of mourning pollution for a deceased lineage member, and extend them with the reasons for abstention based on folk biology. She may well have intercourse on the festival honoring husbands (*Karva Chaut* in Hindi), as is customary, but there may be numerous occasions

during any month when her ritual devotions signal to her husband that tonight should not be the night lest some supernatural
displeasure ensue. A man is usually reluctant to infringe on his
wife's religious scruples, even if he does not share them with the
same intensity. In this way and almost only in this way can a wife
take initiative in regulating intercourse. She can do so without
direct communication about it with her husband. If he should
insist she cannot well refuse, but a woman determined to avoid
the shame of being a pregnant grandmother is triply committed
to intense piety, conscious that it cannot but bring good to her
whole family, because (perhaps less consciously) it is a means of
avoiding conception, and finally because abstinence may be good
for her husband's health.

Discussion between husband and wife about any aspect of their
sexual relations is likely to be minimal. This is not so much because of any all-pervading prudery. Women commonly hear and
may participate in uninhibited talk and jokes about sex with
other women and occasionally with certain men, such as their
husband's younger brother, though women of higher caste rank
are not usually so free in their talk as are women of the lower-
ranked jatis. But in both high and low circles the subject of their
own sex life is not considered proper matter for discussion between husband and wife. One reason is that the man is supposed
to take complete initiative; he might well take any talk about it
as back talk. And he has no need to justify his sexual initiatives
with her—or lack of them. In the popular metaphor, he provides the seed, she the soil.

In Sherupur village, Dr. Ketayun Gould writes, "What the
women stress is not their lack of enjoyment of the sex act once it
starts . . . but their absolute inability to initiate the sexual act,
to refuse it, or to have any say in the prevention of conception"
(1969a:1890). Accounts of similar restraint come from various
parts in India (cf. Dubey and Devgan 1969:69; Poffenberger
1969:110–111; Rao and Mathen 1970:12; Nag 1972:237). A
poignant example is given by Marshall of a childless woman, aged
36, of the low-ranking Chamars, who had been told that conception might occur if she put a pillow under her hips during in-

tercourse. "Asked if she tried it, she replied: 'I couldn't possibly tell my husband I wanted to do that. Though I want children very much, I am too shy to talk about such things with him' " (1972a:145).

Appreciating this shyness, survey workers have tended to shy away from intimate questions or to put them with either too much tact or too little, so that the statistics on the incidence of abstinence seem to be much understated. In the Mysore study, abstinence was found to be the method of family limitation most commonly used; it was reported as the only method used (that is, experienced) by rural women, but only by 2.3% of them. In the sample of Bangalore city women, 9.5% reported using some method, and 6.7% reported using abstinence only (Mysore 1961: 166–167). Among a large sample (16,159) of urban husbands asked if they had ever practiced family limitation by abstinence, 6.7% replied that they had (NSS Number 116, 1967:87). Curiously, there was no regular progression by age groups; 6.5% replied affirmatively in age group 17–21, 6.57% in age group 47–51. Perhaps some of the older men had practiced abstention for fertility limitation but preferred to think that they had been dutifully observing religious mandates. Whatever the reason, the survey statistics so far available seem to give little indication of the real effect that periodic abstention has had on fertility rates. It may well be that this has been the single most important means of fertility control.

The Withdrawal Technique

A method that has been very effectively used in some societies, though it has been of lesser importance among Indian peoples, is coitus interruptus, involving the man's withdrawal during coitus before ejaculation. In his survey of contraceptive techniques around the world, Burton Benedict finds that this is by far the most commonly reported method from primitive societies, that it was a principal method in the West before modern chemical and mechanical resources became available, and that, except in the United States, it remains one of the major contraceptive techniques (Benedict 1970:172). In India, it seems to be used more often among the educated and wealthier than among the poorer and uneducated people.

Some of the Indian surveys that have included questions about this technique indicate that only a small percentage of men and women know of it at all (cf. Mysore 1961:162–163), but the most likely circumstance is that reported from a village of Meerut district. Withdrawal is nearly universally known there as a way of preventing conception, but, as with complete abstinence, it is considered appropriate only for older couples who have married children (Marshall 1972a:153).

Some villagers expressed considerable aversion to this method when family planning workers explained various methods to them in the course of the Singur project in West Bengal. Among 328 couples who were persuaded to accept some method, only 2% to 3% took to coitus interruptus (Mathen 1962:46; Rao and Mathen 1970:35). But the villagers interviewed by Mrs. Uma Guha, also in West Bengal, showed no general aversion, at least among the higher-ranking Sheikh Muslims. Among them, 14 of the 189 "sexually active" women in the sample (7.4%) reported the use of this technique, although only 1 out of 472 women of the lower groups of Muslims did. Among the Hindu women, 10 of 199 (5%) said that they had tried this technique (Nag 1962: 183).[2] And among the Punjabi villagers studied in the Khanna project, "Perhaps 10% of couples had used the method before observations started, though irregularly" (Wyon and Gordon 1971:124). In one of the Khanna villages a special intensive program of family planning teaching and contraceptive supply was conducted for five years. Of several methods explained to the villagers, withdrawal was one that they could accept. "At the last visit to Chakohi in April 1960, 39 per cent of wives aged 15 to 44 years claimed that their husbands had been practicing with-

2. Two other contraceptive measures are known in these villages. One is by taking a bath and washing the vagina after coitus, reported as used by 12.2% of the "sexually active" Sheikh women, 4.5% of the non-Sheikh, and 4.5% of the Hindus. The other is by introducing "a piece of cloth soaked in oil, preferably mustard oil, into the vagina just after coitus." This technique was reported by 4.2% of the Sheikh, 6.6% of the non-Sheikh, and 4.5% of the Hindu women (Nag 1962:58, 183; see also Himes 1963:114–122).

drawal" (*ibid.:*44). How effective coitus interruptus had been in limiting conceptions could not be statistically determined because of the small number of births in the single village.

Educated couples make considerable use of this technique, judging by survey data from Delhi and Calcutta. Agarwala collected data in 1955–58 on 5912 patients who had come into clinics in the Delhi area. Of this number, 3424 couples had practiced some contraceptive method before attending the clinic. About 92% of the husbands were educated up to high school or beyond. The most common method used by these couples before their clinic visits was the condom, used by 56.3%. But withdrawal had been practiced by a considerable number, amounting to 25.8% of those who had used any method (Krishna Murthy 1968:59–60).

In the 1947–49 survey of three samples of Bengali women, two in Calcutta and the third from a rural area, the questioners drew almost a complete blank in the rural area from the 1455 married women they asked about their use of family planning methods. Only four acknowledged any use at all, and these four named abstinence. But in the middle-class section of Beniatola, 13.2% of the women said they had used one or more methods, 100 of 167 reported "husband uses" (i. e., the condom), and 32 reported having used coitus interruptus. In the wealthier Ballygunge section, 37.9% said they had used a method or combination of methods. Among them also the condom was most frequently used, reported by 251 of 551 women; coitus interruptus was reported by 235 of 551 women (Chandrasekaran and George 1962: 83).

A 1965 study of fertility practices in the Chetla area of Calcutta revealed even more use of the withdrawal technique. The women in this sample were not so well educated as those in the sample just mentioned; about 20% of them had been educated to high school or beyond. Among the 964 couples included in this survey, 407 (42.2%) said that they were "practicing family planning" presumably currently, at the time of the inquiry. The method most often reported was coitus interruptus, given by 172, as against 111 reporting use of condoms. It is noteworthy that among those who were trying to limit their fertility, only 37.8%

were using mechanical or chemical devices and 62.2% were using the traditional device-less methods of coitus interruptus, abstinence, and "safe period" (Sen and Sen 1967a:17).

This research entailed an unusual and illuminating feature, a follow-up study in the next year, 1966, to examine the effectiveness of various methods of contraception. In this phase of the study, 182 couples who had said they were using some methods were interviewed again, and their annual pregnancy rate per 100 married women was compared with that of nonusers.[3] The rate among the nonusers was 72.9; it was 29.7 among those who did try some method, including "irregular users." Those few who used an intrauterine device had a very low rate, 1.6. The rate for users of condoms was 26.1 and was significantly lower for the 147 couples who were practicing withdrawal, 17.4 (Sen and Sen 1967b). The couples interviewed in this study were too few, the time span of the project too short, the interviews too brief to yield a firm basis for wide generalization. But the several relevant studies do suggest strongly that the withdrawal technique has been one of the important means of curtailing fertility.

Abortion

The significance of abortion as a method of birth control in India has been estimated by an official body. The report of the committee appointed by the Ministry of Health to study the question of the legalization of abortion offered "some guesses" concerning the magnitude of the practice. The report assumes that "for every 73 live births 25 abortions take place of which 15 are induced" (Report of Committee 1966:18). In other words, out of every 100 pregnancies, 73 result in live births, 10 in natural abortions (miscarriages), 2 presumably in stillbirths, and 15 are terminated by induced abortions. The estimated number of induced abortions per year in India, the report continues, assuming a birth rate of 39 per thousand and a population of 500 million,

3. The annual rate was calculated on the basis of total months of exposure in each woman's married life, with fifteen months deducted for each full-term delivery as a period of no risk, taken as nine months of pregnancy and six months of lactation amenorrhea.

is 3.9 million. The population of India has since grown to more than 547 million; if the birth rate is still taken as 39, the committee's estimate would now come to about 4,200,000 induced abortions in India every year, that is to say, more than there are people in Norway or in New Zealand. This estimate was made despite an old section of the Indian Penal Code that was on the books until a more liberal law was enacted in 1971, which held both the abortionist and the woman legally culpable unless the abortion was performed to save the life of the mother (*ibid.*:35–36).

Information on abortions is difficult to elicit, especially from village women. The Khanna project included an intensive study of fetal wastage; abortion was defined as any pregnancy ending before 28 weeks of gestation, and stillbirth as that of a child born dead after more than 28 weeks (Potter *et al.* 1965c:262). The workers in this study could not get the respondents to report induced abortions separately from spontaneous abortions (though it was done in other surveys) because the women objected to detailed inquiries. The respondents were asked to recount their pregnancy histories, including abortions, and some time later a closer, cross-checked inquiry was made with each woman. Five times more abortions were revealed in the later interviews than had been mentioned in the earlier. The authors believe that even the higher rate is an underestimate (*ibid.*:272).

Village opinion in the Khanna area, as elsewhere in India, is much against induced abortions, but some village women do have them, particularly gravid grandmothers and unmarried girls.[4] In a small North Indian village of 570 people, Marshall notes, there were two unmarried girls who had had abortions in the nearest city within a year (1972a:150). These are the most hushed-up cases; abortions obtained by older women can be discussed a bit

4. Ruth Freed has poignantly recounted (1971) the case of a Brahmin girl in a North Indian village who was discovered to be pregnant before her nuptial rites had been consummated. The shame overwhelmed her father, and he saw no other way out but to kill her and to pretend that she had died a natural death. Village opinion tacitly supported him; although the affair was known to other villagers, it was never reported to the police. Other families in the same predicament find less drastic solutions, and one is abortion.

more readily, at least in general terms. Those few villagers who would discuss abortion with interviewers in the Khanna project mentioned as a reason "the father's and mother's diffidence arising from children in the family old enough to know that the parents must have had sexual intercourse for a pregnancy" (Wyon and Gordon 1971:138). In her interviews with village women in West Bengal, Uma Guha found no Sheikh Muslim woman who would admit to having had an induced abortion, although some were said by others to have had one. Thirty-two of the 524 non-Sheikh Muslim women and 15 of the 237 Hindu women, about 7% of each sample, acknowledged that they had obtained abortions (Nag 1962:58).

One study that focused on the incidence of abortions showed a surprisingly high rate (Gandhigram 1963a, 1963b). It was conducted by members of the Institute of Rural Health and Family Planning, Gandhigram, in a town of Tamil Nadu. One hundred women of the weaver community, ranked there as a middle jati, were interviewed about the pregnancies they had had during the three-year period from January 1960 to January–February 1963. Each woman was between 20 and 40, married, and had had at least two live births.

During this three-year period there had been 105 live births among them and 32 induced abortions, a ratio of 30.4 induced abortions for every 100 live births. The average month of pregnancy when the abortion was managed was reported as 2.7, and so it seems that the reports are, in the main, of real and not imagined pregnancies. The eleven women in the sample who were aged 38–40 had the highest induced abortion rate among the seven age classes. There had been 7 induced abortions and 5 live births among them, a ratio of abortion to births of 140%. One of them also reported having had a spontaneous abortion. For this older group the average number of previous pregnancies before the most recent abortion was 10.1; for the whole sample the average was 7.3. A number of the women had had more than one induced abortion, suggesting to the authors that "The woman who has a successful experience of the first induced abortion is more likely to go in for further induced abortions, than the woman venturing for the first time" (Gandhigram 1963a:27; Mohanty 1968:41–43).

These women named three methods of abortion. The most common, used in 21 of 32 instances, was "by directly introducing a stick with an irritant into the cervix, carried out by a barber midwife." Three abortions were said to have been accomplished by taking medicines obtained from "homeopathic or native doctors"; eight abortions were attributed to "self-administered oral medicines like papayye, jaggery, etc." (Gandhigram 1963a:28). The use of a thin stick by a midwife has also been noted from villages near Baroda and in West Bengal (Poffenberger 1969:27; Nag 1962:58).

Medicaments taken orally to act as abortifacients are usually available to villagers, though their effectiveness may be dubious. Some practitioners of the indigenous Ayurvedic system of medicine have such medicines in their repertoire. A brief account of contraceptive prescriptions in the Ayurvedic literature includes the comment that this literature also contains valuable prescriptions for abortion which are simple, nontoxic, and do not have harmful afteraffects (Prakash 1967). Others who may provide potions for the purpose are local shamans, midwives, and even an occasional priest. In Sherupur village, U. P., Ketayun Gould observes, women who have already given birth six or more times make their own decision to try to have an abortion if they become pregnant again. They can make a unilateral decision because "the folk methods leading to abortion are entirely a woman's world" (1969a:1891).

Educated city women not only have available better resources for abortion but avail themselves of the resources with greater average frequency. A study of 1000 women who had registered with a family planning clinic in New Delhi shows that the abortion rate rises sharply with increased education. There were only 17 women in the sample whose husbands were illiterate. These 17 presumably uneducated women reported that 3.29% of their pregnancies had terminated in abortion (induced abortions were not separated from spontaneous ones). The 366 women whose husbands had had a college education had 10.18% of their pregnancies end with abortion, and for 101 women whose husbands had postgraduate education the figure was 12.32%. In the total sample, abortions were not confined to the later years of marriage at all. The highest percentage of abortions to conceptions, 12.06%, was reported for marriage duration of 15 to 20 years, but the second highest, 10.76%, was given for marriage durations of 5 to 7 years. The women who had practiced some family planning method before coming in to the clinic had a higher rate of abortions (11.65%) than those who had not tried any method before registering (8.87%) (Janmejai 1963).

Similar abortion rates appear in another study of Delhi women, based on the records of 5912 who had come in to family planning clinics in the Delhi area (Agarwala 1962b). Their education level was high; over 90% of the husbands had been educated up to high school or beyond. Among them also there was little difference in abortion rate (induced and spontaneous abortions per 100 pregnancies) by duration of marriage. The abortion rate of these women before they came into the clinics was 10.2, but it nearly doubled, to 20.3, among those who had adopted contraceptive methods prescribed by the clinic.[5] The author comments that this strongly suggests that "those women who use contraceptives get motivated not to have an additional child and when they are burdened with an unwanted pregnancy, some resort to abortion" (*ibid.*:142).

In sum, despite a general condemnation of induced abortion by villagers, it appears that a good many of the older village women and a few of the younger have obtained abortions, generally by crude means. This is probably so among poorer urban women as well. Not only do educated women have a more tolerant view of abortions for others (see Husain 1970a:79), but also a considerable proportion of them undergo abortions at all stages of the reproductive span. In the two Delhi studies cited, educated city women

    5. Two samples of Bombay women gave lower abortion rates, of 6.28 and 6.0. The former figure is from the case-cards of 4514 clients who visited the two clinics of the Contraceptive Testing Unit, Indian Council of Medical Research, during 1959–1969. The latter figure is cited as from a study made at the Family Planning and Research Centre, Bombay (Tipnis and Virkar 1970). A case study of 103 Brahmin women of Nagpur city who had passed the menopause shows 618 births and 61 abortions in their reproductive histories (Rakshit 1962: 153–156).

tend to have a higher abortion rate once they have begun (and have lapsed in) the use of modern contraceptive methods. Kingsley Davis has pointed out that induced abortion is one of the surest ways of controlling reproduction, a method that was a principal factor in the halving of the Japanese birth rate and one that "seems particularly suited to the threshold stage of a population-control program" (1967:732). In the threshold stages of the Indian program, the traditional methods of withdrawal and periods of abstinence can be encouraged at the same time that obstacles to the traditional recourse to abortion are being lowered.

TRADITIONAL AND MODERN RESOURCES
FOR THE NEXT STAGE

THE evidence shows that social context has great bearing on fertility control. It is likely that much of the future effectiveness of the family planning program in India—as in other nations—depends on how well planners and policy-makers can grasp the significance of the social factors and on how skillfully administrators and local workers can utilize them in their day-to-day efforts.

Officials and legislators who are responsible for population policy have to deal with conflicting time pressures. The burden of excessive population is a long-term problem, and a family planning program cannot yield much in the way of material benefit or relief in a few years. Meanwhile political leaders and officials have to cope with myriad urgent problems, a good many of which are exacerbated by the overlarge number of souls already born. Urgent, immediate dilemmas tend to overshadow long-range, fundamental concerns, even though national leaders are often aware that the immediate pinch is only a symptom of a greater, underlying problem. While an effective population policy has to be thought of in terms of generations, it has also to show sufficient results in a five-year planning period so that all involved—electorate, leaders, family planning workers—can get from the programs a just sense of accomplishment. We consider first some of the implications of our review for planning and operation in a five-year span and then for policy direction over the longer term.

Five-Year Plan: Methods and Incentives

Now that the legal barriers in India to safer, surgical abortion have been very considerably lowered, the way is open to make this procedure more readily available to the several million women who, every year, strongly need and want to have abortions. The severe shortage of trained medical personnel, and the restrictions on where a village woman can go and what she can pay, require arrangements designed to overcome these limitations. One possibility is to have medical teams for this purpose stationed at places of the main periodic markets, fairs, and pilgrimages which women customarily attend. As people come to know that a woman's privacy in this matter will be respected, that she will be prepared for the operation in terms she can understand, that aftercare will be readily available, that the operation will be performed with safety and at a cost she can afford, a considerable clientele should appear. Most of the clients from the rural areas will be matrons of the middle- and higher-income levels who have several living children. These women should be able to pay a reasonable fee. A major part of the abortion service might be performed by privately organized medical teams working under governmental supervision. The costs to the woman's family would be little, if any, more than they were when abortions were illegal. The costs to society in illness and deaths will probably be very much less than they were when abortions were prohibited under the antiquated regulations of the old Penal Code.

Women who are poor and uneducated are much less likely to avail themselves of an abortion service; poorer men and women are more inclined to choose sterilization operations, especially if monetary incentives are offered. The promotion of sterilization through vasectomy or tubectomy has been one of the most successful sectors of India's family planning program. As we have noted, more sterilization operations have been performed in India than in all other countries combined (Presser 1970:11–12). The operations have been made available, not only in hospitals and clinics, but also by special medical units established at fairs, in several railway stations, and at "family planning camps." In one month-long camp held in Ernakulam district of Kerala state in 1971, 62,913 vasectomies and 505 tubectomies were performed (Krishnakumar 1971, 1972). Participants and their families were brought into the camp headquarters in Cochin city by bus. Each of the men was medically screened before the operation. The male patients received Rs. 45 in cash and about Rs. 55 in gifts like saris and plastic buckets. Given a free meal and entertainment, the participants were then bussed back to their homes in the district. Those from places outside the district were given train or bus tickets. Arrangements were made to provide aftercare.

The success of this venture was based on intensive planning by district officials, headed by the Collector (the chief administrative officer) for Ernakulam district. Higher officers of the state, both elected and administrative, gave vigorous help. There were 501 committees organized, from the village to the district level, to forward the work of the project. In the camp headquarters,

During the month-long festival, the gaily decorated premises were alive with a constant flux of people. . . . Decorations, banners, exibitions, the permanent theatre for music, puppet shows, films, dance dramas, programs by the State's leading literary figures, and other cultural entertainments twenty-four hours a day, processions, decorated floats, baby shows with prizes for healthy babies of sterilized parents, the lottery, and the attractive gifts combined to create the aura of a traditional Indian festival—a successful medium for any campaign strategy (Krishnakumar 1972:181).

After this project, 25 other vasectomy camps were organized in various parts of the country. Within six months after the Ernakulam success, 645,000 vasectomies had been performed at these camps (ibid.:184). In Gujarat state a different method of conducting the camps was tried. The campaign was decentralized, with more than a thousand camps set up in the state for a two-month period. The cash incentives were higher, ranging from Rs. 65 to 75. Fees were paid to "motivators" who brought in men for the operation; their fees ranged between Rs. 10 and Rs. 20. The Gujarat project resulted in 221,933 vasectomies, more than a third of the total from the new camps and well over the target figure for the state (Thakor and Patel 1972; also see Misra 1973:1771).[1]

1. A report of a local vasectomy camp appeared in the Madurai edition of the *Indian Express* for March 8, 1973 (p. 5). The writer, Malini Khanduri, describes the occasion: "It is a big day for all concerned. The operation itself is of minor significance, the more important part is the trappings, the

One criticism of the sterilization program is that those who undergo the operations already have an average of four to five living children, and so the impact on population growth of this large effort is quite small (Vig 1970; Presser 1970:33; Programme Evaluation 1970:77). In Tamil Nadu, however, where a program of compensatory payment for those accepting sterilization was begun in 1956 and payments for canvassers began in 1959, the acceptors now include a good many younger people. Men and women with many children "have already been contacted to a large extent, and the canvassers have been apparently pushing into a younger stratum of families with fewer children" (Repetto 1971:145–146).[2]

A question raised about sterilization concerns its psychic cost to the individual, especially to younger men and women (Bose 1964). The psychic consequences depend on general cultural attitudes as well as on individual reactions. One attitude favoring vasectomy was expressed in Bankipur village near Meerut; twelve of the forty-three men interviewed on the subject believed that a man who had a vasectomy would be more healthy than other men because he would not lose any of his semen, "the vital fluid that causes men's healthiness and virility" (Marshall 1972a:162). As

---

deals, the bargains and the attractions which make the operation possible. It all began with the award. The award is given to the district which shows the maximum number of family planning operations performed. Our District Commissioner wanted his district to get that award, no matter how."

The account goes on to tell how the Deputy Commissioner had been instructed to let the lower officials know that they had to produce candidates for vasectomy if they wanted to keep their jobs, and how this word passed on from *tehsildars* to *patwaris* to village headmen. In their villages each headman had summoned the men and asked for volunteers. None. "Then the headman very casually asked Bihari: 'Oh, Bihari, that land dispute of yours, it hasn't been settled yet, has it?' Silence. After a while Bihari spoke, 'If I . . . ?' 'Ah, my good man, God will reward you for your wisdom. You are a man after my own heart.'" . . . Jaggu then began to wonder aloud about his tube-well, and Milkha about the fence he wanted to put up. Soon, the writer relates, the village had twenty volunteers. This sketch may be fictional, the general situation it depicts does occur.

2. A follow-up study of 297 men of Madurai district, Tamil Nadu, who had undergone vasectomy gave less favorable results. The average elapsed interval from wife's last pregnancy to time of sterilization was 5.7 years. In this sample, 25% of the men had unfavorable opinions about the operation (Srinivasan and Kachirayan 1968).

against this favorable belief, there is the possibility, statistically rare but socially grave, that a slip by the surgeon or later by a man's wife may leave him with both a presumed vasectomy and a pregnant wife.

Tubectomy for women is, in general, a more certain procedure, though surgically more complicated and costly. To make it an option open to women of poorer families, at least where hospital facilities are available, it is probably best combined with hospital delivery of a woman's births after a certain number, both procedures made attractive by incentive offers. Aftercare is particularly important. A woman in a Punjab village expressed this concern when she told a health worker, "I will have a sterilization, but only because you are living right here in the village and will be available to help if I get into trouble" (C. E. Taylor 1970:114).

Such help has also been needed by many of the women who received an intrauterine device (IUD or "loop") insertion. As a low-cost, easily removed device, the IUD seemed to be the modern method best suited to Indian conditions, especially for the spacing of births. So the Family Planning Programme was vigorously directed toward getting large numbers of women to accept loops. In 1965–66, 810,000 were inserted, and 900,000 during the following year. But, as the UN mission reported, the campaign was pressed too rapidly and with insufficient preparation. The women were not well screened, so that some who were physiologically not suited for the device received them, with unhealthy results. Others had not been adequately warned of the common side effects, such as backaches and, especially, irregular bleedings. Follow-up care was far from adequate, and soon women throughout India were hearing and telling of painful aftereffects, in tales that gained horrifying embellishments in the telling. The number of insertions dropped sharply each year after 1967–68 (UN 1970:7–8).

In Sherupur village, U. P., Ketayun Gould reports, "exaggerated stories regarding bleeding connected with the IUCD arouse untold fears and are a common subject of gossip. . . ." (1969a:1891). The story was told of a woman in another village, sister of one of the village women, who had bled unceasingly for six months after receiving an IUD; in consequence not one woman in Sherupur would accept the device. A physician, Dr. L. E. Blickenstaff, who had worked in several camps for IUD insertions, recounts some of the "atrocity stories" heard by village women about the device, frightful tales that might have been allayed if the woman had been given more explanation about the loop and some realistic instructions about retaining it. He adds examples of occasional deficiencies in the physicians' techniques, of sloppiness under the pressure of meeting target quotas (1967: 32–34).

Despite these deficiencies, the IUD program has had significant impact. One indication of this is given in a study of 2100 Maharashtrian women who had received IUDs at camps in 1965–67 and were interviewed between 1968 and 1970. Their median age at the time of the insertion was 32.5 years, and they had had an average of 4.5 children. The authors, Kumudini Dandekar and Surekha Nikam, note that "the women seemed to adopt the loop for family-limitation rather than for the spacing of children" (1971:2394; also see Programme Evaluation 1970:82). Hence most of them, we may estimate, were from the higher, wealthier groups and were already grandmothers or soon to be. One evidence of their eagerness to limit births is that some 44% of them received loops while they were in a period of postpartum amenorrhea, when another conception was less likely. Some 24% of these women said that they accepted an IUD without having their husband's permission to do so. In 7% of the cases, the husband had brought pressure on the wife to have the device. At the time of the interviews, two to four years after the insertions, 20% of the women in the sample still retained the device and had done so for an average of 36 months. The average period of retention among the whole sample was then about 19 months. Among those whose original loops were no longer in place, 4% had had insertions, 5% relied on condoms, 12% had husbands who had undergone vasectomies, and 31% had had tubectomies. The authors conclude that even with all the shortcomings of the IUD project during 1965–67 in Maharashtra, "it may have prevented many more than 50,000 births in the state" (*ibid.*:2394).

Other studies of IUD acceptors in Maharashtra showed the

women to be, on the average, 30.9 years old at the time of acceptance and to have 3.7 living children (Zakaria 1969:15–18). In the
city area of Greater Bombay, the acceptors were younger, with an
average age of 27 years, and had fewer children; 60% had three
or fewer living children. Muslims were represented among the
acceptors in greater proportion (20%) than their proportion in the
area's population (13%), perhaps because Muslims in this area
tend to be better educated and have higher average income than
in most other parts of India.

In all of India, the number of IUD insertions reported for the
year 1970–71 was 470,000; the total number made previously and
through 1971 was more than 4,100,000. Even allowing for numerical optimism in the reports and short retention periods by some
women, four million insertions must have averted a good many
pregnancies. Considerably more can be averted when basic medical
research on the IUD is extended, when the applications of existing
knowledge are more carefully carried out, and when communication with the receiving women is improved. The IUD can still be
the method of choice for many who are already motivated to stop
having children. If such women find the IUD unsatisfactory, a
good many of them, as the Dandekar and Nikam study indicates,
turn to other modern methods.

The use of condoms has been strongly encouraged by the Family
Planning Programme. The supply and suppliers have been vastly
expanded and the commercial price greatly reduced (about two
cents for a packet of three). In 1968–69 some 50.6 million pieces
were distributed, but the fertility results of this expanded distribution have not as yet been clearly ascertained. The UN Mission
commented, "Scarcely anything is known, however, concerning
the regularity of use and the use-effectiveness of condoms, and
studies of these aspects are much needed" (1970:8).

Other modern contraceptives are not feasible for most Indian
couples. Pills, pessaries, foam tablets, and jellies presume a kind
of affluence or privacy or plumbing that does not exist in the vast
majority of Indian homes.[3] When several modern methods, partic-

3. If the pills could be made widely available at low prices, perhaps
combined with needed vitamins, and taking them associated with a woman's

ularly foam tablets, were made available to couples in the test populations of some experimental projects, a number of the couples who adopted the new methods simply substituted them for the traditional methods. In the Khanna study, some 500 couples reported using the modern methods, but produced no change in birth rates. "A possible explanation was that the introduced contraceptives replaced an earlier practice of folk methods, perhaps equally effective" (Wyon and Gordon 1971:149). Research workers in an experimental project in Bangladesh have suspected that the slight rise in fertility rates after many men began to use condoms occurred because some couples replaced traditional methods with reliance on condoms and were less rigorous in the use of the new method than they had been in the old.

A traditional method that has not yet been given much attention by the Family Planning Programme, and one that could be much more widely and effectively used, is coitus interruptus. It has been and is being used by some couples, as we have noted, but many think that it is not suited for them. Field workers in the Singur project in West Bengal found it difficult to convince doubting villagers of the practicality of this method. Their principal questions had to do with the place where the semen was to be discharged and the effects on the health of the husband and wife practicing this method (Mathen 1962:41). Both questions are based on deep-rooted beliefs of Hinduism. Any bodily secretion, whether saliva, blood, or excretion, becomes ritually dangerous when separated from the body. Contact with such substance, even one's own, defiles a person ritually and therefore restricts or severs the social relations he may have while in a state of pollution. He cannot resume normal relations with man or proper worship of deity until he purifies himself. Some kinds of defilement are easily expunged—a wash will do—but others require complex ritual purification (Mandelbaum 1970:192–205). Spent semen poses a problem of pollution that some people consider to be a more difficult one than that involved in normal sexual relations. The spending of a man's semen, as we have mentioned, is in any event

---

daily worship, this method might well become an effective one for motivated couples.

popularly considered to be a debilitating experience for him and is apparently thought by some to be all the more so in coitus interruptus. Yet there are established means for ritual prophylaxis and purification that could be suggested in advocating the use of this inexpensive, feasible, proven method.

Extending knowledge about birth control methods and improving their feasibility and availability are two necessary parts of a population policy. But they are not sufficient to relieve the nation's population burden adequately because many men and women, particularly among the poorest half of the people, feel no compelling motivation to limit their fertility. The usual family planning package of providing information, supplies, and services has most influence on those of higher income and education who are already motivated to limit their fertility—at least somewhat. But even among such people, the results of pilot and experimental projects have been mixed; some have been quite successful, others not so. The Singur project, to take one example of good results, made contraceptive devices and operations available to 7058 eligible couples in an area some 20 miles northwest of Calcutta. Beginning in 1957, the methods offered were foam tablets and advice on rhythm and withdrawal procedures; condom distribution was begun in 1960; vasectomy operations were made available in 1962, IUDs in 1965, and tubectomies in 1966. By the end of 1968, 33.4% of the eligible couples had accepted contraceptive measures. Among the acceptors, 27.4% had had operations, 24% of the women had had IUD insertions, and 30.4% of the couples reported using condoms. In one of the five units in the project area, the birth rate had declined from 42.3 per 1000 in 1963 to 35.0 in 1968, and the pregnancy rate there was 29.2 for contraceptive users as against 81.7 for those who were not using contraceptives (Saha 1971; see Ross et. al. 1972:7, for estimates of the effectiveness of other projects).

Some experimental projects have reported much less favorable results. Thus when Kumudini Dandekar conducted a program in a town near Poona during 1959–61, the project workers directed their efforts to 1255 eligible women. When the project ended, there were only 18 users of contraceptive devices among them, and the average duration of use was 16 months (1967:67). A survey in the Comilla–Kotwali *thana* of East Pakistan (now Bangladesh) was done in 1968 to assess the effects of a family planning project that had been in operation since 1964. Only 4% of the women in a sample of 1600 said that they or their husbands were using contraceptive methods. The authors note that, because of under-reporting, the percentages of users is probably about 6%, but "the corrected proportion of users is still substantially low enough that any impact upon fertility will be minimal" (Stoeckel and Choudhury 1971:129).

The report of the Khanna study concludes that "The availability of more efficient methods of birth control had precipitated no rush to utilize them." The authors note that by 1969, when the study was ended, the government Family Planning Programme had established clinics, surgical centers, and condom distributors throughout the state. This "provided new methods of birth control for old, but offered little else to modify the total circumstance in which the Punjabis considered and decided the merits not only of method, but how much birth control to apply" (Wyon and Gordon 1971:312–313). But this comment does not allow for the time it takes for people to shift their fertility standards; it does not take into account the authors' own observations of the sharp rise in age of marriage for girls; and it underplays other indications of lowering fertility rates in this prospering region. To be sure, prospering families may not reduce their fertility enough to meet the nation's need, but they tend in time to be motivated toward some control and, importantly, toward more education for their children.

Among families of the poorer half, certainly of the poorer third, no such development is now in view. Their poverty is not necessarily caused by their high fertility, but their fertility helps shackle many of them to poverty. It is possible that in time the general economic condition of the country will improve enough to raise the level of the poorest to the point where they would reduce their average fertility. But, as Prime Minister Indira Gandhi has said, the people of India "cannot afford to wait" (1969:5).

To persuade the poorer people quickly, special inducements are needed, and the most effective so far have been gifts of money and goods to men who get vasectomies, as the Ernakulam and Gujarat projects show. When a committee set up by the Ministry of Health and Family Planning reported in 1968 on proposed incentives and disincentives affecting fertility, they stated that compensation for sterilization or IUD insertion "is for meeting out-of-pocket expenses and is not an incentive as such" (Small Family Norm Committee 1968:16). Though some national leaders find the idea of monetary incentives repugnant (cf. Narayan 1968:15), program administrators have not worried much about having compensation for expenses merge into financial incentive. While compensation for clients and for canvassers has led to many administrative and other difficulties, these programs have succeeded, as we have noted, in having millions of men and women sterilized—10.2 million through 1971, according to official count (Report of Ministry 1972: see also Program Memorandum 1968:142–151; Humberger 1969:51–96).

This effort does reach the poor. In a Bombay project, 61% of the men who had the operation lived in slum areas; 61% were also illiterate, and 58% were unskilled workers (Zakaria 1969:14). In Madras city, Dr. P. G. Krishnan found that of 1000 men who had vasectomies, 57% reported incomes of less than Rs. 50 per month, and 96% of the sample reported less than Rs. 100 (Repetto 1971:152). Of those who had vasectomies in the Ernakulam camp of 1971, 59% were agricultural laborers and unskilled workers, 65.9% had little or no formal education (Krishnakumar 1971:152–153).

The Report of the Small Family Norm Committee in 1968 recommended a series of disincentives, such as disadvantages for families with more than three children, withdrawal of financial concessions, and demerits in getting government positions. Some of these disincentives have been tried (cf. Zakaria 1969), but if they are to be effective they require greater supervision than India's budget or administrative apparatus can yet afford. The Committee also recommended raising the minimum legal age at marriage. This measure may be a useful one for lowering fertility at a later stage of India's administrative development, but it is not likely to have a beneficial effect in the near future.

The Sarda Act of 1929, which set the minimum legal age of marriage for girls at 14, had very mixed results. The Hindu Code Bill of 1956 raised that minimum age to 15. It seems very likely that raising the minimum legal age to a level that would be effective in curtailing fertility rates—say age 20—would arouse great opposition, would result in widespread evasion, would bring on great burdens in enforcement, and might seriously damage the public's view of the Family Planning Programme.

More promising proposals are those designed for a particular group, such as a set of workers who share common job interests and have a union organization. One of the best of these has been proposed by Ronald Ridker for women workers on tea plantations. Estate managements usually maintain good records, provide medical facilities, and want to reduce the birth rate among their women workers for the sake of the estate's efficiency and profitability. The proposal is to set up a joint savings account in the name of the company and of the woman. The company would pay a certain amount into this account during each month that the woman is not pregnant. If she does become pregnant she forfeits a substantial amount of the sum that the company had credited to her, though she is eligible to begin accumulating savings again after delivery. She becomes full owner of the account when she has passed through her childbearing years. This plan is attractive to the companies because they would save on the maternity and child care benefits that they are legally obligated to pay. Many companies also have had to cope with the problem of too many children and unemployed teenagers on the estates. The women who reduced their fertility would benefit by having a handsome sum for their later years (Ridker 1969b, 1971). Some plan of this kind might be suitable for the Indian Railways and other large employers (cf. Bhattacharyya 1969; Lewis 1970:26). And if the Indian government decides to embark on massive public works projects for rural employment, as recommended by Dandekar and Rath (1971), and as discussed in a Planning Commission paper (1972), it would be additionally beneficial for the purposes intended if some family planning qualification were required of those so employed.

Personnel

The effectiveness of the people professionally engaged in family planning work is a critical matter, and certain kinds of professionals, who would seem to be well suited to family planning work, turn out to have only limited usefulness. Others, who have not so far been drawn into the program, may be able to make very significant contributions.

Qualified physicians and nurses are obviously essential for certain parts of a family planning program, but they are in such drastically short supply that their contributions are best focused on services that only they can perform, such as sterilization operations. Moreover, their selection and training do not favor the kind of close rapport with villagers that is required for effective family planning communication. Ashish Bose has commented (1970a: 326) that medical doctors "cannot be viewed as the main agents of social change in India." And Kingsley Davis has deplored the tendency in all countries to designate population control as a medical or public health task. "The categorization assures popular support because it puts population policy in the hands of respected medical personnel, but, by the same token, it gives responsibility for leadership to people who think in terms of clinics and patients, of pills and IUDs, and who bring to the handling of economic and social phenomena a self-confident naiveté" (1967:733). In India there are good reasons on behalf of population policy for greatly increasing the number of nurses and doctors, especially of women doctors, but their sheer scarcity over the next decades requires that many family planning tasks be done by paramedical and nonmedical personnel (cf. Rice 1968).

A traditional paramedical profession found everywhere in South Asia is that of *dai*, midwife. Midwives attend more than half of all deliveries (see NSS Number 175, 1970:15) and would seem to be suited for recruitment to family planning work by reason of their craft. However, efforts to recruit them, especially by the family planning program in Pakistan, have not been very successful. In describing the results of a dai field organization, in which some 36,500 dais were employed on salary and additional fees, the Pakistan Commissioner for Family Planning reported that their most useful service was as "communicators of the family planning message." Their actual recruiting of IUD acceptors and their services as distributors of contraceptives were not up to expectations. A UN Mission recommended that the dais be replaced by better trained and qualified fulltime workers (Ahmad 1971:7, 13; see also Croley *et. al.* 1966; Jafarey *et. al.* 1968). An intensive experimental project, carried on during a four-year period with 70 dais in Lahore did not yield good results. More than 30 of the 70 dais dropped out before the end of the period, and most of the rest were not satisfied with doing family planning work, nor were they particularly good at it (Gardezi and Inayatullah 1969). In India, also, efforts to enlist dais into family planning work have floundered (Program Memorandum 1968:77–79; Lal 1969; Poffenberger 1969:26).

One reason for these failures is that the dai's work is considered by villagers to be an unclean chore that someone has to do. Those who do it for pay are usually among the poorest, least educated women of low status and little prestige. Among Muslims, many of the dais are destitute widows who work for whatever small fees they can get. Among Hindus, they are usually from the low-ranking groups (Mandelbaum 1970:190). Childbirth is considered a polluting experience for all involved in it, especially among Hindus. Those who attend and help for reasons of kinship or charity can purify themselves by ritual means. But women who attend as part of their group's customary occupation and for pay are, by that reason, consigned to low-caste status. Most dais do not have the education or the self-confidence to act as liaison between government agencies and villagers, nor are villagers likely to give much serious attention to what a dai might have to recommend.[4]

4. There is probably an important difference between men and women in their attitude toward dais. Dr. Doranne Jacobson has written (in a personal communication) that women may be more receptive to dais than men are. Men may find indigenous medical practitioners more approachable than doctors, but village women might not find a male medical practitioner of any sort approachable, particularly if he is an older male in her husband's

Held in quite different repute by their neighbors are the practitioners of indigenous systems of medicine. They are usually respected residents of their towns and villages, more approachable, less expensive, more readily understood than are most doctors trained in scientific medicine. There are several ancient systems, Ayurveda, Unani, and Siddha being the best known. Their practitioners are estimated to number some 400,000, and they constitute the large majority of all medical practitioners in the country. A nationwide sample of medical practitioners in rural areas showed 5.25% to be graduates of schools of scientific (allopathic) medicine; another 16.8% were licentiates and others who practiced allopathic medicine; and 77.9% practiced other systems of curing, mostly the traditional methods but also including some homeopathic practitioners (NSS Number 172, 1970:3; Program Memorandum 1968:82–84).

The traditional pharmacopoeias contain prescriptions for contraceptive and abortifacient drugs (Prakash 1967); a good many indigenous practitioners supplement these with modern drugs, often administered by injection (see, e.g., Poffenberger and Poffenburger 1973). But their effectiveness in fertility control seems to be low. It could be much improved if careful evaluations of their drugs were made and the best combination of the old and the new methods worked out and applied. These practitioners can be reached through their own professional and trade contacts. They have customarily been consulted by women with fertility problems, including those who want to stop having children; they could provide dependable advice to young couples and could treat many of those who experience uncomfortable aftereffects of IUD insertion or of sterilization.

This vast pool of health practitioners has as yet been little tapped for family planning purposes. A beginning was made in 1967 to enlist Ayurvedic medical colleges in research on contraceptive drugs and to persuade their faculties to include family planning in their curriculums. Few investments in family planning give promise of higher returns than a strong effort to reach

village. In North India especially, a young woman is expected to conduct herself with respectful avoidance of such a man.

and advise the indigenous practitioners and to reward them for successful efforts in fertility control. Political leaders have sensed the importance to villagers of the indigenous practitioners who live among them and are in tune with their ways. Government subsidies, of relatively modest amounts, have been allocated to help their colleges and professional organizations. But the historic antipathy of scientific medicine to other systems may make it very difficult for medically trained administrators to recognize the great potential contribution that indigenous practitioners can contribute to this program.

Even less acceptable to modern professionals but also of great potential service to family planning are the shamans. These are men, and occasionally women, who are believed to be able to summon supernatural beings, who can be possessed by a spirit and speak with its voice to answer questions put by suffering, anxious, or distressed people (see Kakar 1972; Mandelbaum 1972). The questions have to do with illness and other personal difficulties, especially with the failure to have a son. An assistant to a popular shaman in Sagar district of Madhya Pradesh told an anthropologist, "There are too many kids in India; the population is growing out of bounds, and people are starving to death. But people come to the god [who speaks through the shaman] mostly for one reason: they want kids" (Jacobson 1970:371; also see Opler 1964: 207).

The voice that speaks through the shaman (he is called *bhagat* in Hindi) may counsel ritual offerings or penitential acts or dietary taboos or may even refer the questioner to an allopathic practitioner. The ailments that people bring to shamans seem often to be the result of intolerable social–psychological pressures. Shamans perform important therapeutic functions by helping their clients to reconcile, under transnatural directives, conflicting forces in and around them. There is scarcely a village in India without a shaman or one within easy reach.

The familiar spirits are usually local deities, some of them directly concerned with human fertility. Hence some shamans in a village near Baroda were not enthusiastic about family planning, claiming that "the use of Government-offered methods might offend deities of fertility and health, the mother goddesses" (Poffenberger and Poffenberger 1973). But shamans are not necessarily opposed to birth control. There are three in the small village of Bunkipur near Meerut, who in addition to giving counsel through their inspirational mode, can also provide recipes for abortifacients (Marshall 1972a:154).

Shamans are now consulted about fertility problems; they could help encourage fertility control and, especially, could help to allay conflicts and anxieties experienced by some of those who have been sterilized. Relief from psychic conflict is what villagers commonly seek from shamans, and their counsel frequently enough does lead to relief. Most of the shamans I have known impressed me as sincere believers in the transnatural sources of their inspiration. The successful ones also tend to be shrewd judges of personality and sensitive observers of their local scene. What a shaman pronounces in his trancelike state of dissociation is not entirely dissociated from his mundane judgments. It could be of considerable benefit to the national effort if reliable information about family planning was particularly directed to shamans and they were encouraged to take a benign view of it. Messages about fertility flow through thousands of shamans to millions of their clients; it would be well if their potential were recognized in some of the directives that stream down from the higher echelons of the Programme's administration.

Reaching the village shaman with the Programme's resources may arouse uncomfortable conflict in a planner's mind and will certainly require special approaches in planning. The shaman's professional contacts are personal and not with earthly organizations. Though he may well have keen intelligence, he may have little or no formal schooling. Yet shamans can be identified in their villages and towns; they can be encouraged to attend family planning festivals, especially if held at major shrines that are considered particularly congenial to their own familiar spirits. A first step in this process could be taken by those trustees of major shrines who recognize that the purposes of religion are at one with the nation's welfare in the matter of population. If they could find means of presenting this imperative cause in the sacred precincts, a way might be opened for bringing the strength of religion to the difficult decisions about modern contraceptive methods.

All these suggestions have long-range implications, but all can be launched, with reasonable promise of effective results, within an immediate plan period. They are intended to utilize the social and cultural forces that actually animate people rather than to ignore these forces or antagonize the people. Thought should also be given to the social needs and actual motivations of those who are employed by the Programme, a subject that is mentioned in the next chapter on long-term considerations.

SIX

THE LONGER PERSPECTIVE

Evaluations

APPRAISALS of the Programme usually take the macroview, use aggregate statistical data, broadly survey the national effort. A few studies take the microview, explore what has been happening in specific villages and neighborhoods, try to explain the behavior of real persons. The two are complementary and both are useful. But each approach raises a different set of questions and tends toward differing emphases in planning.

Among the overall surveys, we have already noted the 1970 report of the UN Mission and the 1970 report of the Programme Evaluation Organisation of the Planning Commission.[1] In addition to these official documents, the monograph-length appraisal by George B. Simmons (1971) and the brief account by A. R. Kamat (1971) are particularly cogent.

The two official reports highlight the administrative shortcomings in personnel matters. The Programme Evaluation report tells that in the districts sampled, only two-thirds of the posts sanctioned were filled at the time of the survey, that liaison with related medical and public health agencies was tenuous, and that training was so limited that the "majority of the staff attended only short orientation courses of 3 to 7 days duration" (1970:2, 4). The UN Mission noted similar defects of training and administrative organization, and recommended quick remedial action (1970:16–17). These defects, to be sure, were partly the result of ambitious targets that required a vast new governmental apparatus within a few years. But the agency was created, is functioning,

1. The field work for the former was done during January–March 1969, and for the latter in two three-month periods just before and just after the UN field work period.

and, in the nature of governmental agencies, will in time come to fill its slots and regularize its training procedures.

Simmons' study *The Indian Investment in Family Planning* also emphasizes problems of personnel. He observes that probably the most important shortage faced by the Programme is "the lack of sufficient trained personnel at all levels" (1971:154). His own field research of IUD and sterilization acceptors in Haryana state found that most of them had been actively recruited by workers and that the acceptors might not have used any methods of fertility control otherwise. So the shortage of workers is a serious bottleneck (*ibid.*:107–108). But Simmons also questions the existing administrative apparatus which is lamentably hampered by defects of bureaucracies in general and those of Indian bureaucracy in particular. He points out that workers, especially those of the lower echelons, are underpaid, have little hope of getting extra rewards for extra work, and once appointed are firmly ensconced in the job regardless of their efficiency or lack of it. The average extension worker does not work particularly long or arduous hours, and his productivity is low, more because of the faults of the system than of the individual workers. Simmons suggests ways of building better incentives into the administrative system and means of supplementing it through the use of canvassers, of private practitioners, and of business organizations (*ibid.*:163–165). He concludes that despite the inefficiencies of the administrative system, the Programme's efforts have generated considerable benefit to the nation. His calculations put the ratio of benefits to costs at a very high level. For every rupee invested in family planning between 1956 and 1970, the return in savings to the national economy per year was never lower than 39.1 rupees (1957–58); in 1967–68 the benefit-cost ratio was 88.1. "Often the unimpressive impact of the Program on the total rate of population growth makes one forget that the percentage decline in the birth rate is not the only measure of the Program's success" (*ibid.*: 93–94; also see Misra 1973:1771–1772).

One major deficiency that is deplored in all these survey evaluations and is succinctly put by Kamat (1971:726) is the lack of basic information about what kinds of people do or do not take to contraceptive methods, why some do and what happens to them if they do, and where family planning workers can most effectively direct their efforts. The UN Mission recommended increased research on motivation and communication, and urged that all efforts should be made to utilize such research (1970:17). The Programme Evaluation report also advised that research on family planning communication and "levels of persuasibility" be done and that research results be quickly applied (1970:5–11). Simmons noted that information has a high economic value and that special priority should be given to studies of public response to alternative methods of fertility control (1971:195–197).

The information so sorely needed cannot well be procured through the limited questions, the brief encounters, the stiff interviews of the usual survey procedures. It takes longer acquaintance, closer observation, informal conversations, and good rapport to develop an understanding of what is entailed in people's fertility behavior. After such understandings are built up from studies of a number of places and groups, the ideas generated by them can *then* be tested statistically over a wide scene by survey methods.

One study that does present a close view of fertility determinants was done in 1968–69 by John F. Marshall in a village he calls Bunkipur, situated not far from Meerut city, some forty miles north of Delhi. Marshall chose to work in this village of 570 people because he could study conditions before the villagers were directly influenced by a formal, focused family planning program and could observe the first six months of that program's activities. To what degree the Bunkipur villagers are statistically typical was not an issue in this study; what does emerge is a vivid depiction of the fertility behavior, outlook, and problems of actual persons. These are quite congruent with the general Indian trends that we have already noted.

There were supposed to be nine government employees with duties in Bunkipur whose responsibilities included aiding the work of the Family Planning Programme. Two of the nine jobs were unfilled at the time of the study; the influence of the seven employed was minimal. For several, family planning advice was quite peripheral to their regular jobs and beyond their competence. The two female schoolteachers, who lived in Meerut city, spent very little time in the village outside of school hours. They knew few of the villagers and perhaps less about contraception, even though they were supposed to help disseminate family planning information. Similar responsibility was assigned to the official who collected taxes and kept the land records and to the Village Level Worker of the Community Development Programme. Neither did anything about it.

Primary responsibility for family planning work in Bunkipur was on the four positions assigned by health and family planning agencies, of which two had no incumbents because of lapses in recruiting. An Auxiliary Nurse Midwife was employed, but she "was an unmarried urban girl with a profound distaste for, and some fear of, village life." Although Bunkipur was one of the villages she was supposed to visit regularly, she did not come at any time during the year of the study. The woman who was the Family Welfare Worker did not visit Bunkipur either, until she appeared to follow up the intensive phase of the program in the village.

The one official who did something relevant was the Secretary of the *Panchayat,* a council for five villages including Bunkipur. In 1967 he was obliged to recruit forty men for vasectomy from the five villages or possibly lose his job. Having little alternative, "he concentrated his efforts on the more malleable lower *jātis,* primarily Chamars, and cajoled, threatened, pleaded, and bargained, stressing that a fifteen rupee payment (equivalent to four or five days of salary for most landless laborers) would be given for the operation at the family planning center" (1972a:157). From Bunkipur he recruited six poor men, five of them widowers over 60 years old and one a 35-year-old Chamar, who had a daughter and three sons, to whom he promised the job of Vice-Chairman of the Panchayat. This man, as it turned out, was the only one to suffer painful aftereffects and was the case which became a warning example to others in the village.

The inactivity of the other government workers was not necessarily a great loss at the time because many of the Bunkipur villagers then viewed government officials with some misgivings and tended to be timid when officials came bearing contraceptive gifts. Moreover, a villager who wanted to have a sterilization operation or an IUD insertion had to make at least one trip out of the village to a hospital, clinic, or private doctor. And in Bunkipur, Marshall writes, there was then "the almost universal belief that clinics and hospitals were time-consuming, corrupt, humiliating, and frequently ineffectual places" (*ibid.*:363, 285; 1972b: 25).

Yet there were six couples in the reproductive years who, unbeknownst to most of the other villagers, had adopted modern methods; to these six was added the well-known case of the unfortunate aspirant to the vice-chairmanship. Five of the six were of the landowning Thakur group. Two men, aged 34 and 45, both with several children, had had vasectomies because of their wives' insistence. One man claimed to have used condoms, though only occasionally. Two women had had IUD insertions (one later removed), and one woman had undergone tubectomy (*ibid.*:158– 159). So of the 88 married women in their reproductive years in Bunkipur at the time of the study, seven were protected against pregnancy by modern methods.

The villagers of Bunkipur, Marshall observes, are not inherently hostile to innovations in their lives; many of them have adopted other new ways. In case of illness, those who can afford to consult modern doctors do so despite their mistrust of hospitals and clinics. But the weight of their experience and reason, as we have seen to be true for many in India, counts against much curtailment of fertility. For one matter, they believed (in 1968–69) that population growth was good, especially for their own group, because greater numbers can mean more influence, and more power can lead to better standards of living. Children cost parents very little and the rewards of having many sons are considerable. These villagers are reluctant to forgo the benefit of having more sons because they have small margin for risk, little or no cushion for misfortune (*ibid.*:138–140, 328; 1972b:27).

To most of the villagers, family planning meant chiefly vasectomy, and many of them told Marshall of their fears about the possible physiological and sexual effects of the operation. They were also concerned, as we have noted in other settings, that a vasectomized man might be deeply disgraced if his wife should later turn out to have become pregnant. And they suspected that some women with tubectomies or IUDs might become more sexually insouciant than respectable wives should be (1972a:289, 299–300, 292–293).

At the very first formal family planning meeting in Bunkipur an elder pungently said, "In village Rampur a man had three sons and was sterilized. Six months later all his children died in an epidemic, but he can't have any more. What do you do about that, Doctor-Sahib?" (Marshall 1972a:319). The leaders in the village could not then do much to advocate family planning. The cause was not popular; supporting it might call their own credibility into question, as happened to a Chamar leader when it became known that he had been paid for his advocacy. There was nothing in it for the leaders (Marshall 1972a:303; see also Programme Evaluation 1970:6; Mencher 1970:38).

To be effective in Bunkipur, Marshall concludes, family planning workers would have to be able to distinguish the relevant subgroups in the village, focus on at least one representative of each subgroup, and recognize what kinds of people were at all open to persuasion. Not open to any such persuasion were the 47 married women (among the 88 who were aged 45 or less) who had no son or only one living son.[2] Seven of the 88 eligible women were already "protected." There were seven others who seemed to merit first priority in the family planning workers' attention because each of them had no special reason for resisting birth control.

Among the eligible women who were disinclined to take the family planning message personally, there were three who were more than 40 years old and so thought themselves beyond conception. Four Muslim wives, among the eight Muslim families,

2. One needed another daughter because marriages in her jati require the groom's family to pay bride price to the bride's family. If her three sons were to be suitably married, her family needed the income of more bride price than her one living daughter would bring.

were forbidden by their husbands to listen to talk about family planning. The largest number of potential adopters who paid little or no attention to the program activities when they were begun in Bunkipur were the 20 women who were either pregnant then or within 18 months of having given birth and so thought themselves to be still impregnable.

Some of these 20, Marshall notes, could be shifted from the category of "do not/can" to the category of those who can and do practice fertility control. To induce them to do so would require accessible knowledge, supplies, medical facilities, and "a minimum of persuasive appeals." The more difficult task would be to shift those who are in the "do not/cannot" category, those who feel that they cannot possibly accept family planning for any or all of the reasons we have noted. Changing their views will require long-term effort (Marshall 1972a:355–362).

The priorities for the next planning period implied in close studies like that of Bunkipur differ from those proposed in the survey evaluations. There seems to be little urgency about appointing another Auxiliary Nurse Midwife in the Bunkipur vicinity; she might turn out to be like the one who is mentally allergic to villages and villagers. Nor is better liaison between the Community Development Programme and the Family Planning Programme so imperative if tighter liaison only results in a directive to the Village Level Worker that would add yet another assignment to his already impossibly long list of duties.

Suggested improvements may take on a different appearance when viewed from the perspective of the villager rather than from that of headquarters. For example, several of the evaluations recommend a considerable increase in the number of jeeps assigned to the Programme (see Program Memorandum 1968:iv; UN Mission 1970:15; Programme Evaluation 1970:31). These vehicles do indeed diminish physical distances, but they also tend to increase the social distances between official and villager. The machines undoubtedly contribute to the prestige and morale of the officers who command them, but they may be counterproductive for the purposes of the program as well as being expensive. Maintenance costs are very high; one estimate is that about a third of all Family Planning Programme vehicles are out of service at any one time. An official of the Programme can probably accomplish more for family planning if he rides buses or even bicycles or country transport, and if he keeps talking to people en route, than if he whizzes in his jeep from village to village on hurried tours of inspection.

Expanded training programs may do little good if they do not direct the trainees in what they need to know and do in order to be effective for family planning. They need to learn enough about the people, whether in a village like Bunkipur or in a city neighborhood, to tell what kinds of people are likely to respond to what types of appeal. They should be trained to see to it that those who have accepted sterilization or the IUD get competent aftercare, that they are reassured when worried, and that false rumors are countered.[3] They should learn to utilize the local social networks that influence each person's views and acts. There are networks of kin and jati, of religion and devotion, of markets and trade, of patrons and politics. Every villager and townsman is bound into several networks. Through them he receives and imparts information; within them he derives and gives value judgments. In each network there are likely to be key persons whose reach and influence are relatively great and who, if they themselves are persuaded of the benefits of family planning, might well convince others. It is asking a good deal of Family Planning Workers, constrained as they are by limitations of incentive, time, social insight, and official dignity, to seek out such persons, but a training program could guide and encourage them to do so.

Though fertility can be markedly reduced over a planning period with the means that are already at hand or nearly so, the kind of massive reduction that is the goal of the program will re-

3. The Programme Evaluation report gives figures on the proportion of acceptors in the sample who thought that their health had deteriorated as a result of their acceptance. Calculations from the data that are provided indicate that some 26% of the sample of men who had had vasectomies reported that they suffered impaired health, 28% of the tubectomy cases so reported, and 48% of the women who had had IUD insertions (1970:97). Such high proportions suggest the possibility of considerable public antagonism developing against IUD and sterilization if remedial measures are not taken.

quire long-range measures that will help shift the relevant social attitudes and cultural conditions.

Investment in the Education of Girls

There is at least one measure within the feasible scope of policy-makers that would have important long-run effects in decreasing fertility rates in India. It is to increase education for girls greatly, with emphasis on education in health and family planning. We have noted above how effectively the education of girls decreases the number of children they have as married women. While the decrease in earlier generations of educated women may not be exactly duplicated in future generations—those who were educated then were a highly selected set—there is little question that educated women will continue to bear fewer children than do uneducated women. "Along with the general progress of education," A. R. Kamat states, "it is the education of women which is crucial for the success of the family planning programers in the predominantly rural societies" (1971:726). We have also noted how strong a desire there is in very many Indian families to educate their boys and, as they succeed in doing so, to find educated girls as suitable wives for the educated boys. There are indeed some who oppose educating girls at all, and many more who would object to providing equal educational opportunities for each sex. But if planning decisions were made to keep the education of girls at a par with that of boys, if additional places for girls were made available, if special incentives to educate girls were offered, it is likely that greater equality in educational attendance would quickly develop.

Two major decisions of educational policy would have to be made to bring this about. One is to halt the present trend toward favoring much more education for boys than for girls. The other is to change the school curriculum so that health and family planning become a major subject of study from the primary school on, with increasing specialization in the subject for girls in the middle and secondary grades. Arriving at such decisions will require much discussion at central, state, and local levels; implementing them in the classroom will be a complex task at all levels. But as a long-range measure this seems to be both feasible and well calculated to help toward the reduction of fertility and to bring public benefit in other ways as well.

At all age levels, far smaller percentages of girls than of boys are in school. The all-India figures for 1965–66 showed that in the 11–14 age group, 16.5% of the girls and 34.2% of the boys were enrolled, and at ages 14–17, 6.9% of the girls and 11.5% of the boys were enrolled. These were enrollment figures; the actual attendance was probably less, especially for the girls (Poffenberger 1971:171; Kamat 1972:1230). A 1972 paper of the Planning Commission projects that the sharp differences in the proportion of boys and girls in school will continue. The paper proposes large increases in education but concedes that even by the end of the Fifth Plan, in 1979, perhaps only half or less of the girls aged 11–14 will be in school. The constraints, according to the Commission, "are mostly social and the non-availability of women teachers in adequate numbers" (Approach to the Fifth Plan 1972:1108).

The "social" constraints are presumably those having to do with the general objections to educating girls to a level equal to or near that of their future husbands. Such objections do pose moral and political, as well as social, problems but a good many Indian parents might respond favorably if they came to realize that giving educational advantages to their daughters would, in time, bring great advantages to the children these daughters will eventually rear. As for the stated difficulty of providing sufficient women teachers, the recent increase in girls' education, small as the total proportion of educated girls still is, should soon provide a sufficient pool of potential teachers.[4]

After such decisions are implemented, significant fertility reductions should appear within a decade, with continuing and accelerated reductions subsequently. Not only would the greater

4. A social problem that troubles school administrators is the greater degree of absenteeism and personnel turnover among women than among men teachers. The difference is due mainly to family responsibilities, but this constraint could be eased by providing more generously for the special familial needs of women teachers.

number of educated wives have fewer children but they would probably help influence their less educated kin and neighbors toward family planning.

Curriculum development in health and family planning will have to be worked out carefully in each state and district, but the very presence of this concentration through much of the students' school years is likely to have a significant effect in itself. Observations in a village near Baroda indicate that students in the eleventh standard are much more aware of the family planning message than might be expected. "During their maturing years they had seen family planning posters and slogans in public places and had been aware of announcements and references in films and newspapers that related to the problem of excessive family size" (Poffenberger 1971:174). Poffenberger has described the disappointing turnout for a family planning film that was shown in this village. The audience was small, many were children, and the official who spoke after the film showing could scarcely be heard because of the noise made by the large number of children in the audience (1969:31–32). But though the speaker's words were lost on the children, the film's message may have reached them and they may have learned that family planning was a subject that could and should be discussed. Those who hear discussions of fertility, physiology, and family planning in their school years will probably have quite a different attitude toward these subjects than do those who learn nothing about them or hear only uncertain rumors during their schooling.

It will be particularly important in this educational effort to bring girls of the poorer groups into school and to keep them there. Although plans for educating children of these groups have not had much success so far, it may be easier to keep their girls in school than their boys, since the girls tend to be less restive, at least in primary and middle grades, and under less pressure to contribute early to the family's income. A relatively small national expenditure for new kinds of incentives for the education of such girls, in addition to those that are already available, might well bring notable increases in their school attendance.

Girls whose education has been focused on health and family planning will provide good candidates for the growing number of health service positions at every level of skill. If emphasis is given to recruiting women, the proportion of women among medical and paramedical personnel could rise to approximate the proportions in the Soviet Union, where some 80% of the doctors are women.

Political Opposition and Countervailing Forces

Policy decisions of this kind cannot long remain isolated from political debate. Indeed, the whole subject of family planning seems likely to become much more drawn into partisan controversy than it was in the early stages of the Programme. Although some scholars and political leaders have expressed hope that this vital subject could be kept out of the turbulent political arena (Bose 1970a; Weiner 1970:8), it has already been opposed on partisan grounds. The Shiv Sena party of Maharashtra has openly argued against family planning for its adherents; other local or communal party leaders have expressed antagonism to it (Weiner 1970:10–11; Poffenberger 1973:26). The Hindu Temple Protection Committee of Madurai has sponsored protests against family planning; one large meeting was addressed by officers of the Jana Sangh party. Similar protests are reported from Tirunelveli and other places. Two mahants, religious leaders, of Raipur have conducted fasts against family planning (The *Sunday Standard*, Coimbatore, February 25, 1973, p. 7; the *Indian Express*, Madurai, January 22, 1973, p. 7; February 20, 1973, p. 8).

Indira Gandhi has directly challenged such opposition. In her address to a family planning conference she said, "There is propaganda in the effect that the family planning programme will upset the relative population ratios of the various groups in our country and thus weaken the political power or bargaining position of these groups. This pernicious doctrine may well convince people because of its very fallacy" (1969:5–6).

That fallacy, however, is deeply rooted. The low-ranking Chamars of the little village of Bunkipur, for example, feel strongly that with growing numbers they will gain growing power and advantage in the village, even though they are now the most numerous group and about the most disadvantaged. Chamar leaders who work in Meerut city "rarely disclosed accurately or positively what they learned about contraception—in part because to them family planning meant a method of reducing the numbers and power of their caste" (Marshall 1972b:28). That idea is held in wider social circles and at ascending political levels, not only in India but in many nations (see Berelson 1969:4–6). It is an aspect of the contradiction we have noted between private or local interest and the public, national welfare.

This issue is likely to be debated vigorously in India for a good many years and through successive changes in the Indian political scene. In a sense the population question transcends political change, even radical change, since the leaders of whatever kind of government comes to power will have to deal with the burdens resulting from too many babies being born. One political approach to the problem may yield greater success than another, but all will have to take account of the villager's and townsman's own outlook. Open political controversy, for all its failings, can be a great means of public education on critical issues. Perhaps the growing political debate on the subject in India may help toward building a public awareness that may in time help to bring fertility rates down to levels healthier for the body politic.

But in this debate who is to uphold the side of nationwide welfare, or public interest? Elected officials must serve their constituencies and on many matters a politician's constituents are likely to press him to look after their local and private interests. No matter how well a legislator understands the nation's dire need for reduced fertility, he can scarcely view with dispassion the prospect of his own group's numerical decline on the voting rolls (Weiner 1971:599–600). All the more so when grants of funds from the central government to the states and localities are calibrated, as they have been, on the basis of population.

There are indeed statesmen, eminent authorities, respected personalities, government officials, writers, as well as civic-minded local figures who have and will defend the whole national interest in the matter of family planning. Yet continual, concerted political defense needs organization outside the governmental administration, full-time workers, steady funds.

The existing voluntary agencies that engage in family planning work or are sympathetic to it have been suggested as a possible source for such a political-educational push (Program Memorandum 1968:90–91; Bose 1970a: 326; Programme Evaluation 1970:28). These agencies range from national societies like the Indian Red Cross and the Family Planning Association to welfare organizations such as Mahila Samaj, to clinics such as those organized by the Indian Women's Aid Society. But their efforts have been so limited and diffuse, their workers so few, their funds so small as to make them appear restricted to doing local good deeds rather than being capable of national political influence. Yet they have potential for great influence. They could draw in, to a much greater degree than they have so far, many well-educated women, wives of men influential in their professions, businesses, official positions. The household duties of these women do not absorb their full energies or intelligence. The family planning cause is one they can understand in their bones and many of them are capable of persevering, dedicated service to it. Some of these women are superb organizers; some are very close to men who wield the levers of power. True, these levers cannot quickly overturn deep popular reluctance toward having few children but the women can urge the men to make decisions, such as that for girls' education, which will help move people closer to effective fertility management. What is needed to strengthen this potential force is a drive to increase the appeal and expand the membership of these voluntary agencies. Funds are needed for full-time workers to provide a steady frame for the volunteer efforts. Private individuals and endowments committed to the advance of family planning could not make better use of their resources than to help a resurgent voluntary movement that would become strong enough to plead the nation's cause in population matters in the face of rising opposition.

A General View

Viewed in worldwide demographic perspective, population growth in India is quite like that experienced by other developing societies. It is at the phase where mortality rates have declined sharply while fertility rates still remain high. Modern means of lowering mortality, such as inoculations, meet with little or no opposition when people become convinced that the techniques do good and not harm. Further, as Agarwala has pointed out, the death rate can be greatly reduced "without any substantial modification of the social structure and without the actual involvement of the people in the programme. But this cannot be said about fertility" (1966a:143). If population increase is to be checked in a contemporary society, the people must become involved in the effort, and they must change at least some of their previous social and cultural patterns.

Humankind in both tribal and civilized societies has long engaged in customary practices that keep their numbers below the biological maximum of reproduction, as Steven Polgar has shown (1972:210). At the present juncture of cultural evolution, it is governments that are expected to protect and improve the people's standards of living, and so government leaders in many countries are charged with bringing about whatever changes are required to alleviate the dangers of rapidly increasing population. In his three-volume study of the poverty of nations, Myrdal concludes that the population explosion itself is the most important change that has taken place in South Asia since World War II, and he hopefully adds that the spread of birth control will be the greatest change in the next few decades, "making reforms and development easier to accomplish" (1968:1530).

The initial groundwork for this spread in India has been well begun through the Family Planning Programme. Despite its deficiencies, a large administrative agency has been established, an industrial, distributional, and medical infrastructure has been built, public awareness of family planning has vastly increased, and millions of men and women have accepted ways of controlling their fertility. Cost-benefit calculations indicate that substantial savings to the nation have already been made by the investment in family planning.

The evidence suggests, as we have noted above, that in the next stages of the program more emphasis should be given to the social conditions of particular groups and categories and not so much to nationwide targets and broadside, hard-sell campaigns. Women and men who are inclined toward fertility control for traditional reasons should receive special attention. Mothers who have recently given birth should be reached with reliable information on birth spacing. Major efforts should be directed to giving them and their babies the kind of care that will lower infant and child mortality and so eventually lower fertility (see Chandrasekhar 1972). Women in their thirties who are actual or imminent grandmothers should be recognized as being keenly interested in fertility control. Family planning information should cover such traditional methods as abstinence, coitus interruptus, and abortion as well as modern techniques of preventing conception.

Those who accept IUD or sterilization require regular after-care and social support, both for their own health and to prevent an even greater backlash against those methods than has so far arisen. Such care and support can best be given by persons of the same locality and social level. For these and other family planning purposes, the great number of indigenous practitioners and shamans could provide important resources. Though many individuals have accepted sterilization or IUD insertion at the urging of paid canvassers, the influence of motivators, paid or unpaid, would be more general and solid if they were persons who were respected in particular social networks, such as in jati councils, caste associations, sects, village Panchayats. A possible additional support for men and women who have been sterilized, especially among the very poor, would be to give them preference for employment in large government projects. These suggestions and others like them are best tested in pilot projects before being implemented through the nation. But pilot projects can only be useful if their progress is carefully followed, if evaluations are regularly made, and if information about their results becomes known to all who are responsibly involved in planning.

The evidence further suggests that certain measures proposed to curtail fertility would do little good. Legislation to raise the legal age at marriage would not do much to lower fertility at this juncture; the imposition of penalties and disincentives for large families is not practicable and would arouse great opposition.

In the long run, development and fertility control are mutually reinforcing; the more there is of one, the greater the possibility of the other. Both purposes would be advanced by much greater investment in the education of girls. Considerable improvement in the content of education in India has been urged by officials and nonofficials alike. But whatever the deficiencies of the present system, girls who have been educated in it beyond the early primary grades consistently show lower average fertility after they marry than do their age mates of similar social-economic status but of less education. When the educational experience is improved, and especially if students regularly study much more about health and family planning than they do now, the impact of education in lowering fertility should be all the greater.

Governmental efforts toward fertility reduction must cope with certain dilemmas. One of them, as has been seen, is that those babies who are a planner's worry are also a parent's hope and joy. Another principal dilemma is that the measures practicable in the short run are not sufficient to meet the nation's problem in the long run. Demographers who criticize existing programs in almost all developing nations are quite right in saying that the plans so far are, at best, only tentative first steps toward effective fertility control. But the planners and politicians are also right in sensing the limits of what they can propose by way of shaking people's deep emotions about their fertility. Emotions are rooted in cultural and social experience. If family planning workers can learn how to utilize that experience effectively, the nation's welfare in population matters will be well served.

BIBLIOGRAPHY

Agarwala, S. N. 1962a. Age at marriage in India. Allahabad: Kitab Mahal.

——. 1962b. "A study of abortion rates—socio-economic and other factors," *Family Planning News* 3(6):139–142.

——. 1962c. *Attitude towards family planning in India.* Delhi: Institute of Economic Growth.

——. 1964. "Social and cultural factors affecting fertility in India," *Population Review* 8:73–78.

——. 1966a. *Some problems of India's population.* Bombay: Vora and Co. Publishers Private Ltd.

——. 1966b. "Raising the marriage age for women: a means to lower the birth rate," *Economic and Political Weekly* 1:797–798.

——. 1967a. "Widow remarriages in some rural areas of northern India," *Demography* 4:126–134.

——. 1967b. *Population.* New Delhi: National Book Trust.

——. 1968. "Widowhood age and length of fertile union in India," in *World views of population problems.* Edited by Egon Szabady, pp. 11–16. Budapest: Akademiai Kiado.

——. 1970. *A demographic study of six urbanizing villages.* New York: Asia Publishing House.

——. 1971. "Three or two or one or none," *Illustrated Weekly of India* 97(6):6–11.

Ahmad, Wajihuddin. 1971. "Field structures in family planning," *Studies in Family Planning* 2:6–13.

Aitken, Annie, and John Stoeckel. 1971. "Dynamics of the Muslim–Hindu differential in family planning practices in rural East Pakistan," *Social Biology* 18:268–276.

Aiyar, Swaminathan S. 1971. "What the census reveals," *Times of India,* May 7, 1971, p. 10.

"Approach to the Fifth Plan." 1972. *Economic and Political Weekly* 7:1107–1110.

Bebarta, Prafulla Chandra. 1961. "Recent studies in fertility," *Sociological Bulletin* 10:27–41.

———. 1966. "Family type and fertility: a study in six Delhi villages," *Economic and Political Weekly* 1:633–634.

Benedict, Burton. 1970. "Population regulation in primitive societies," in *Population Control*. Edited by Anthony Allison, pp. 165–180. Baltimore: Penguin Books.

———. 1973. "Other people's family planning," *Science* 180:1045–1046.

Berelson, Bernard. 1969. "Before Family Planning." *Studies in Family Planning*, no. 38, pp. 1–15.

Bhate, Vaijayanti. 1964. "Decline in mortality and changes in age at marriage as factors affecting incidence of widowhood," *Artha Vijnana* 6:92–104.

Bhattacharyya, S. K. 1969. "Family planning in the railways," *Journal of Family Welfare* 15(3):31–36.

Blake, Judith. 1965. "Demographic science and the redirection of population policy," in *Public health and population change*. Edited by Mindel Sheps and Jeanne C. Ridley, pp. 41–69. Pittsburgh: University of Pittsburgh Press.

Blickenstaff, Leonard E. 1967. "Sociology of family planning," *Journal of the Christian Medical Association of India* 42:31–36.

Bogue, Donald J. 1962. "Some tentative recommendations for a 'sociologically correct' family planning comunication and motivation program in India," *Research in Family planning*. Edited by Clyde V. Kiser, pp. 503–538. Princeton: Princeton University Press.

Bose, Ashish. 1964. "Cost calculations not enough," *Economic Weekly* 16:1449–1450.

———. 1970a. "Eleven myths of family planning," *South Asian Review* 3:323–330.

———. 1970b. "Demographic research in India: 1947–1969," in *Studies in demography*. Compiled by A. Bose, P. B. Desai ,and P. S. Jain, pp. 17–49. Chapel Hill: University of North Carolina Press.

Burch, Thomas K., and Murray Gendell. 1971. "Extended family structure and fertility: some conceptual and methodological issues," in *Culture and population*. Edited by S. Polgar, pp. 87–104. Carolina Population Center, Monograph 9. Cambridge, Mass.: Schenkman.

Carstairs, G. Morris. 1957. *The twice-born: a study of a community of high-caste Hindus.* London: Hogarth Press.

Chandra Sekhar, A. 1971. *Census of India 1971, provisional population totals, supplement.* Series I, India, Paper 1 of 1971, supplement. New Delhi: Office of the Registrar General.

Chandrasekaran, C. 1952. "Cultural patterns in relation to family planning in India," in *Report of the proceedings, third international conference on planned parenthood, 22–29 November, 1952, Bombay, India,* pp. 73–79. Bombay: Family Planning Association of India.

Chandrasekaran, C., and M. V. George. 1952. "Mechanisms underlying the differences in fertility patterns of Bengalee women from three socio-economic groups," *Milbank Memorial Fund Quarterly* 40:59–89.

Chandrasekhar, S. 1953. "The prospect of planned parenthood in India," *Pacific Affairs* 26:318–328.

———. 1959. "Family planning in an Indian village: motives and methods," *Population Review* 3:63–71.

———. 1969. "India's family planning programme: what we have accomplished so far," *Journal of Family Welfare* 15(3):10–14.

———. 1972. *Infant mortality, population growth, and family planning in India.* London: George Allen and Unwin.

Chaudhury, Rafique Huda. 1971. "Differential fertility by religious group in East Pakistan," *Social Biology* 18:188–191.

Chidambaram, V. C. 1967. "Raising the female age at marriage in India: a demographer's dilemma," in *Implications of raising the female age at marriage in India.* Edited by Demographic Training and Research Centre, pp. 35–47. Bombay: DTRC.

Croley, H. T., S. Z. Haider, Sultana Begum, and Harold C. Gustafson. 1966. "Characteristics and utilization of midwives in a selected rural area of East Pakistan," *Demography* 3:578–580.

Dandekar, Kumudini. 1959. *Demographic survey of six rural communities.* Publication 37, Gokhale Institute of Politics and Economics, Poona. Bombay: Asia Publishing House.

———. 1967. *Communication in family planning.* New York: Asia Publishing House.

———, and Surekha Nikam. 1971. "What did fail? Loop (IUCD) as a contraceptive? Administrators of loop programme? Or, our ill-conceived expectations?" *Economic and Political Weekly* 6:2392–2394.

Dandekar, V. M., and Nilakantha Rath. 1971. "Poverty in India," *Economic and Political Weekly* 6:25–48, 106–146.

Dasgupta, Biplab. 1970. "Population policy: the crucial factor," *South Asian Review* 3:331–346.

Datta, Subodh, 1961. "Differential fertility in West Bengal in 1956," *Artha Vijnana* 3:67–82.

Davis, Kingsley. 1946. "Human fertility in India," *American Journal of Sociology* 52:243–254.

———. 1951. *The population of India and Pakistan*. Princeton: Princeton University Press.

———. 1967. "Population policy: will current programs succeed?" *Science* 158:730–739.

Department of Family Planning. 1969. *Programme information (1969–70)*. New Delhi: Department of Family Planning.

Dheer, R. S. 1964. "Emphasize motivation, not means," *Economic Weekly* 16:1503.

Dhillon, H. S. 1970. *Status of women in India and implications for family planning programme*. Technical Series 9; reference no. 45. New Delhi: Central Health Education Bureau.

Driver, Edwin D. 1963. *Differential fertility in India*. Princeton: Princeton University Press.

Dubey, D. C., and A. K. Devgan. 1969. *Family planning communications studies in India*. New Delhi: Central Family Planning Institute.

El-Badry, M. A. 1967. "A study of differential fertility in Bombay," *Demography* 4:626–640.

Freed, R. S. 1971. "The legal process in a village of north India: the case of Maya," *Transactions of the New York Academy of Sciences* 33:423–435.

Gandhi, Indira. 1969. "Inaugural address at the sixth all-India conference on family planning," *Journal of Family Welfare* 15(3):3–6.

Gandhi, M. K. 1947. *Self-restraint v. self-indulgence*. Ahmedabad: Navajivan Publishing House.

———. 1962. *Birth control*. Edited by A. T. Hingorani. Bombay: Bharatiya Vidya Bhavan.

Gandhigram. 1963a. "A report on the study of the incidence of abortions in a weaver community in the project area," *Bulletin of the Pilot Health Project, Gandhigram* 4(3):24–30.

———. 1963b. "A brief report on the base line survey on attitude, knowledge and practice in family planning in a few selected villages in the project area," *Bulletin of the Pilot Health Project, Gandhigram* 4(3):14–23.

Gardezi, Hassan N., and Attiya Inayatullah. 1969. *The dai study: the dai-midwife—a local functionary and her role in family plan-*

ning. Lahore, Pakistan: West Pakistan Family Planning Association.

Gould, Ketayun H. 1969a. "Sex and contraception in Sherupur: family planning in a north Indian village," *Economic and Political Weekly* 4:1887–1892.

———. 1969b. "Family planning: a politically suicidal issue," *Economic and Political Weekly* 4:1513–1518.

———. 1972a. "Comments," *Current Anthropology* 13:249–250.

———. 1972b. "Parsis and urban demography: some research possibilities," *Journal of Marriage and the Family* (May 1972), pp. 345–352.

Govind, S. 1970. "New dimensions to family planning programme," *Thought* 22(38):24–25.

Gupta, Raghuraj. 1965. "Cultural factors in birth rate reduction in rural communities of UP," *Family Planning News* 6(2):2–6.

Hall, Roberta L. 1972. "The demographic transition: stage four," *Current Anthropology* 13:212–215.

Hashmi, Sultan S. 1965. "The people of Karachi: demographic characteristics," *Monographs in the Economics of Development*, no. 13. Karachi: Pakistan Institute of Development Economics.

Hauser, Philip. 1967. "Family planning and population programs," *Demography* 4:397–414. (Review)

Hawthorn, Geoffrey. 1970. *The sociology of fertility*. London: Collier-Macmillan.

Himes, N. E. 1963. *The medical history of contraception*. New York: Gamut Press (original edition 1936).

Humberger, Edward M. 1969. *Incentives in the ecology and adoption of family planning in rural India*. New Delhi: Ford Foundation. (Mimeographed)

Husain, I. Z. 1970a. *An urban fertility field: a report on city of Lucknow*. Lucknow: Demographic Research Centre.

———. 1970b. "Educational status and differential fertility in India," *Social Biology* 17:132–139.

Jacobson, Doranne. 1970. "Hidden faces." Unpublished Ph.D. dissertation, Department of Anthropology, Columbia University.

Jafarey, S. A., J. Gilbert Hardee, and A. P. Satterthwaite. 1968. "Use of medical–paramedical personnel and traditional midwives in the Pakistan family planning program," *Demography* 5:666–678.

Jain, S. P. 1967a. "State growth rates and their components," in *Patterns of population change in India*. Edited by Ashish Bose, pp. 13–32. Calcutta: Allied Publishers.

——. 1967b. "Post-partum amenorrhea in Indian women," in *Contributed papers, Sydney Conference, International Union for the Scientific Study of Population*, pp. 378–388.

Janmejai, Krishna. 1963. "Socio-economic aspects of abortion," *Family Planning News* 4(3):55–57.

Kakar, D. N. 1972. "The health centre doctor and spirit medium in a north Indian village," *Eastern Anthropologist* 25:249–258.

Kale, B. D. 1969. Family planning resurvey in Dharwar. Dharwar: Demographic Research Centre.

Kamat, A. R. 1971. "Family planning programmes: a reassessment," *Economic and Political Weekly* 6:723–727.

——. 1972. "The educational situation," *Economic and Political Weekly* 7:1229–1237.

Kapil, Krishan K., and Devandra N. Saksena. 1968. "A bibliography of family planning knowledge, attitude, and practice studies in India, 1951–68." *Newsletter,* issue no. 26, pp. 19–38. Bombay: Demographic Training and Research Centre.

Kar, S. B. 1968. *A review of research needs in family planning.* Technical Series 4. New Delhi: Central Health Education Bureau. [Reprinted from the *Journal of Family Welfare* 15(3):23–40].

Karkal, Malini. 1968. "Age at marriage," *Journal of Family Welfare* 14(3):51–56.

——. 1971. "Cultural factors influencing fertility: post-partum abstention from sexual intercourse," *Man in India* 51:15–26.

Kaur, S., and John Edlefson. 1968. *Some observations regarding KAP (knowledge, attitudes and practices related to family planning) research in India.* New Delhi: U.S. Agency for International Development.

Kirk, Dudley. 1966. "Factors affecting Moslem natality," in *Family planning and population programs.* Edited by B. Berelson *et al.*, pp. 561–579. Chicago: University of Chicago Press.

Kolenda, Pauline Mahar. 1964. "Religious anxiety and Hindu fate," *Journal of Asian Studies* 23:71–82.

Kripalani, Gul B., Pramala Maitra, and Tapati Bose. 1971. "Education and its relation to family planning," *Journal of Family Welfare* 18:3–8.

Krishna Murthy, K. G. 1968. *Research in family planning in India.* Delhi: Sterling Publishers.

Krishnakumar, S. 1971. *The story of the Ernakulam experiment in family planning.* Cochin: Government of Kerala.

——. 1972. "Kerala's pioneering experiment in massive vasectomy camps," *Studies in Family Planning* 3:177–185.

Kurtkoti, Shakuntala. 1970. "Planned parenthood is far off in Kelgiri village," *Family Planning News* 11(45):11–13.

Kurup, R. S., and N. V. George. 1969. "Variation in fertility between two generations," *Journal of Family Welfare* 15:31–41.

Lal, Amrit. 1969. "The midwife in family planning," *Yojana* 13(20):21.

Lall, M. M. 1973. "Family planning programme," *Indian Express* (Madurai), February 9, 1973, p. 6.

Lapham, Robert J., and W. Parker Mauldin. 1972. "National family planning programs: review and evaluation," *Studies in Family Planning* 3:29–52.

Learmonth, A. T. A. 1958. "Medical geography in Indo-Pakistan: a study of twenty years' data for the former British India," *Indian Geographical Journal* 32:1–59.

Lewis, John P. 1970. "Population control in India," *Population Bulletin* 26:12–31.

Madalgi, S. S. 1971. "Poverty in India: a comment," *Economic and Political Weekly* 6:503–506.

Mamdani, Mahmood. 1972. *The myth of population control: family, caste, and class in an Indian village.* New York: Monthly Review Press.

Mandelbaum, David G. 1949. "Population problem in India and Pakistan," *Far Eastern Survey* 18:283–287.

——. 1954. "Fertility of early years of marriage in India." Reprinted from *Ghurye Felicitation Volume.* Bombay: Gem Printing Works.

——. 1970. *Society in India*, Vols. I and II. Berkeley and Los Angeles: University of California Press.

——. 1972. "Curing and religion in South Asia," *Journal of the Indian Anthropological Society* 4:1–21.

Marshall, John F. 1972a. "Culture and contraception: response determinants to a family planning program in a North Indian village." Unpublished Ph.D. dissertation, Department of Anthropology, University of Hawaii.

——. 1972b. "Some 'meanings' of family planning to an Indian villager," *Research Previews, University of North Carolina* 19:24–29.

Mathen, K. K. 1962. "Preliminary lessons learned from the rural population control study of Singur," in *Research in Family Planning.* Edited by Clyde V. Kiser, pp. 33–49. Princeton: Princeton University Press.

———. 1965. "The impact of the family planning movement on the Indian population," in *Papers contributed by Indian authors to the world population conference, Belgrade, Yugoslavia, 30 August–10 September*, pp. 287–290. Delhi: Office of the Registrar General.

May, David A., and David M. Heer. 1968. "Son survivorship motivation and family size in India: a computer simulation," *Population Studies* 22:199–210.

Medhora, Phinze B. 1971. "Poverty in India: a comment," *Economic and Political Weekly* 6:543–546.

Mencher, Joan. 1970. "Family planning in India: the role of class values," *Family Planning Perspectives* 2:35–39.

Minkler, Meredith. 1970. "Fertility and female labour force participation in India: a survey of workers in old Delhi area," *Journal of Family Welfare* 17(1):31–43.

Minturn, Leigh, and John T. Hitchcock. 1966. *The Rajputs of Khalapur, India*. New York: John Wiley.

Misra, Bhaskar D. 1973. "Family planning: differential performance of states," *Economic and Political Weekly* 8:1769–1779.

Mohanty, S. P. 1968. "A review of some selected studies on abortion in India," *Journal of Family Welfare* 14(4):39–48.

Montagu, M. F. Ashley. 1957. *The reproductive development of the female*. New York: Julian Press (second edition).

Morrison, William A. 1961. "Family planning attitudes of industrial workers of Ambarnath, a city of western India: a comparative analysis," *Population Studies* 14:235–248.

Myrdal, Gunnar. 1968. *Asian drama: an enquiry into the poverty of nations*. New York: Pantheon.

Mysore. 1961. *The Mysore Population Study: a cooperative project of the United Nations and the Government of India*. New York: United Nations, Department of Economic and Social Affairs.

Nag, Moni. 1962. "Factors affecting human fertility in nonindustrial societies: a cross-cultural study," *Yale University Publications in Anthropology*, no. 66.

———. 1965. "Family type and fertility," in *Papers contributed by Indian authors to the World Population Conference, Belgrade, Yugoslavia, 30 August–10 September*, pp. 131–138. New Delhi: Office of the Registrar General.

———. 1972. "Sex, culture, and human fertility: India and the United States," *Current Anthropology* 13:231–237, 260–263.

Namboodiri, N. Krishnan. 1968. "The changing population of

Kerala." *Monograph No. 7, Census of India, 1961.* New Delhi: Office of the Registrar General.

Narayan, Jayaprakash. 1968. *Our population problem and the need for family planning.* New Delhi: Ministry of Health, Family Planning and Urban Development. (Pamphlet)

Nath, Kamla. 1965. "Women in the new village," *Economic Weekly* 17:813–816.

National Sample Survey. 1962. "Seventh round: October 1953–March 1954." Number 54. Vital notes. Delhi: Manager of Publications.

National Sample Survey. 1967. "Sixteenth round: July 1960–June 1961." No. 116. Tables with notes on family planning. Delhi: Manager of Publications.

National Sample Survey. 1970. "Seventeenth round: September 1961–July 1962." No. 154. Tables with notes on couple fertility. Delhi: Manager of Publications.

National Sample Survey. 1970. "Eighteenth round: February 1963–January 1964." No. 172. Tables with notes on Indian villages: some important results. Delhi: Manager of Publications.

National Sample Survey. 1970. "Eighteenth round: February 1963–January 1964." No. 175. Tables with notes on differential fertility and mortality rates in India. Delhi: Manager of Publications.

National Sample Survey. 1970. "Nineteenth round: July 1964–June 1965." No. 177. Vital rates in India. Delhi: Manager of Publications.

National Sample Survey. 1970. "Nineteenth round: July 1964–June 1965." No. 186. Tables with notes on differential fertility and mortality rates in rural and urban areas of India: Delhi: Manager of Publications.

Nehru, Jawaharlal. 1965. *Nehru: the first sixty years.* Vol. II. Edited by Dorothy Norman. New York: John Day.

Newman, Peter. 1965. *Malaria eradication and population growth.* Bureau of Public Health Economics Research Series, No. 10. Ann Arbor: School of Public Health, University of Michigan.

Nortman, Dorothy L. 1972. "Status of national family planning programmes of developing countries in relation to demographic targets," *Population Studies* 26:5–18.

Oberg, Jenifer. 1971. "Natality in a rural village in northern Chile," in *Culture and population.* Edited by S. Polgar, pp. 124–138. Cambridge, Mass.: Schenkman.

Opler, Morris E. 1964. "Cultural context and population control programs in village India," in *Fact and theory in social science.* Edited by Earl W. Count and Gordon Bowles, pp. 201–221. Syracuse: Syracuse University Press.

Pakrasi, Kanti, and Chittaranjan Malaker. 1967. "The relationship between family type and fertility," *Milbank Memorial Fund Quarterly* 45:451–460.

Pathare, Rajani. 1966. "The family planning programme: a sociological analysis," *Sociological Bulletin* 15(2):44–62.

Paulus, Caleb R. 1966. *The impact of urbanization on fertility in India*. Mysore: Prasaranga, University of Mysore.

Planalp, Jack M. 1971. "Heat stress and culture in North India, *Special Technical Report*, U.S. Army Research Institute of Environmental Medicine.

Poffenberger, Thomas. 1968. "Motivational aspects of resistance to family planning in an Indian village," *Demography* 5:757–766.

———. 1969. *Husband-wife communication and motivation aspects of population control in an Indian village*. Monograph Series 10. New Delhi: Central Family Planning Institute.

———. 1971. "Population learning and out-of-school youth in India," *Studies in Family Planning* 2:171–174.

———, and Shirley B. Poffenberger. 1973. "The social psychology of fertility behavior in a village in India," in *Psychological perspectives on population*. Edited by James Fawcett. New York: Basic Books.

Polgar, Steven. 1972. "Population history and population policies from an anthropological perspective," *Current Anthropology* 13: 203–211.

Pool, D. Ian. 1972. "Comments," *Current Anthropology* 13:252–253.

Population Bulletin. 1970. "India: a bleak demographic future," *Population Bulletin* 26:2–12.

Potter, Robert G., Mary L. New, John B. Wyon, John E. Gordon. 1965a. "A fertility differential in eleven Punjab villages," *Milbank Memorial Fund Quarterly* 43:185–199.

———. 1965b. "Applications of field studies to research on the physiology of human reproduction: lactation and its effects upon birth intervals in eleven Punjab villages, India," in *Public health and population change*. Edited by Mindel C. Sheps and Jeanne Clare Ridley, pp. 377–399. Pittsburgh: University of Pittsburgh Press.

———. 1965c. "Fetal wastage in eleven Punjab villages," *Human Biology* 37:262–273.

Prakash, Surya. 1967. "Ayurveda can help family planning," *Yojana* 11(23):27.

Presser, Harriet B. 1970. "Voluntary sterilization: a world view," *Reports on Population/Family Planning*, no. 5. New York: Population Council and International Institute for the Study of Human Reproduction, Columbia University.

Programme Evaluation Organisation, Planning Commission, Government of India. 1970. *Family planning programme: an evaluation.* New Delhi: Department of Family Planning.

Program Memorandum. 1968. *Family planning: the GOI program.* Agency for International Development, U.S. Department of State.

Rakshit, Sipra. 1962. "Reproductive life of some Maharashtrian Brahmin women," *Man in India* 42:139–159.

Rao, M. N., and K. K. Mathen. 1970. *Rural field study of population control, Singur (1957–1969).* Calcutta: All-India Institute of Hygiene and Public Health.

Raphael, Dana. 1972. "Comments," *Current Anthropology* 13:253–254.

Rele, J. R. 1962. "Some aspects of family and fertility in India," *Population Studies* 15:267–278.

———. 1963. "Fertility differentials in India," *Milbank Memorial Fund Quarterly* 41:183–197.

Report of the committee to study the question of the legislation of abortion. 1966. New Delhi: Ministry of Health and Family Planning.

Report of the Ministry of Health and Family Planning for 1971–72. 1972. Abstracted in *Economic and Political Weekly* 7:997.

Repetto, Robert C. 1971. *Time in India's development programmes.* Cambridge: Harvard University Press.

Rice, Donald T. 1968. "Manpower and training problems in family planning programs," *Demography* 5:767–772.

Ridker, Ronald G. 1969a. "Desired family size and the efficacy of current family planning programs," *Population Studies* 23:279–284.

———. 1969b. "Synopsis of a proposal for a family planning bond," *Studies in Family Planning*, no. 43.

———. 1971. "Savings accounts for family planning: an illustration from the tea estates of India," *Studies in Family Planning* 2:150–152.

Ross, John A., A. Germain, J. E. Forrest, and J. Van Ginneken. 1972. "Findings from family planning research." *Reports on Population/Family Planning*, no. 12. New York: Population Council and International Institute for the Study of Human Reproduction, Columbia University.

Saha, H. 1971. "An evaluation of a family planning programme in a rural area of West Bengal," *Journal of Family Welfare* 18:10–15.

Saxena, G. B. 1965. "Differential fertility in rural Hindu community: a sample survey of the rural Uttar Pradesh, India," *Eugenics Quarterly* 12(3):137–145.

Seghal, B. S., and R. Singh. 1967. "Breast feeding, amenorrhea, and rates of conception in women," *Journal of Family Welfare* 14(1): 44–49.

Sen, Mukta, and D. K. Sen. 1967a. "Family planning practice of couples of reproductive age group in a selected locality in Calcutta–June 1965," *Journal of Family Welfare* 14(1):13–24.

———. 1967b. "Study of contraception without device," *Family Planning News* 8(10):5–6.

Sen, Tulika. 1953. "Reproductive life of some Indian women," *Man in India* 33:31–54.

Sengupta, A. 1965. "A study of the rhythm method in exploring the patterns of libido in the human female," *Journal of Family Welfare* 11(3):47–67.

Shetty, S. N. 1971. "Trends in per capita food availability," *Financial Express* (January 28, 1971), p. 4.

Simmons, George B. 1971. *The Indian investment in family planning.* New York: Population Council.

Small Family Norm Committee. 1968. *Report.* New Delhi: Department of Family Planning.

Sovani, N. V. 1952. "The problem of fertility control in India: cultural factors and development of policy," in *Approaches to problems of high fertility in agrarian societies,* pp. 62–73. New York: Milbank Memorial Fund.

Srinivasan, K. 1967. "A prospective study of the fertility behavior of a group of married women in rural India: design and findings of the first round of enquiry," *Population Review* 11:46–60.

———, and M. Kachirayan. 1968. "Vasectomy follow-up study: findings and implications." *Institute Bulletin, Gandhigram* 5:13–32.

Stoeckel, John, and Moqbul A. Choudhury. 1969a. "Differential fertility in a rural area of East Pakistan," *Milbank Memorial Fund Quarterly* 47:189–198.

———. 1969b. "Factors related to knowledge and practice of family planning in East Pakistani villages," *Social Biology* 16:29–38.

———. 1971. "Family planning knowledge, attitudes, and practice in a rural area of East Pakistan," *International Review of Sociology* 1:122–132.

———, and A. K. M. Alauddan Choudhury. 1971. "Seasonal variation and births in rural East Pakistan," *Journal of Biosocial Science* 3:107–116.

Straus, Murray A., and Dorethea Winkelman. 1969. "Social class, fertility, and authority in nuclear and joint households in Bombay," *Journal of Asian and African Studies* 9:61–74.

Talwar, Prem P. 1965. "Adolescent sterility in an Indian population," *Human Biology* 37:256–261.

——. 1967. "A note on changes in age at marriage of females and their effect on the birth rate in India," *Eugenics Quarterly* 14:291–295.

Taylor, Carl E. 1968. "The health sciences and Indian village culture," in *Science and the human condition in India and Pakistan*. Edited by Ward Morehouse, pp. 153–161. New York: Rockefeller University Press.

——. 1970. "Population trends in an Indian village," *Scientific American* 223:106–114.

Taylor, Richard W. 1969. "Hindu religious values and family planning," *Religion and Society* 16:6–22.

Thakor, V. H., and Vinod M. Patel. 1972. "The Gujarat state massive vasectomy campaign," *Studies in Family Planning* 3:186–192.

Thapar, Savitri. 1965. "Fertility rates and intervals between births in a population in Delhi," in *Papers contributed by Indian authors to the World Population Conference, Belgrade, Yugoslavia, 30 August– 10 September*, pp. 139–143. New Delhi: Office of the Registrar General.

Tipnis, G., and K. D. Virkar. 1970. "A ten-year analysis of cases visiting family planning clinics, *Journal of Family Welfare* 17(2):3–8.

Tripathi, B. D. 1969. "Hindu family system and family planning," *Journal of Social Research* 12:71–78.

United Nations. Advisory Mission to the Government of India. 1969. *An evaluation of the Family Planning Programme of the Government of India*, Document No. TAO/IND/50. New York: United Nations, Department of Economic and Social Affairs, Commissioner for Technical Cooperation.

United Nations. Advisory Mission. 1970. "India: UN mission evaluation of family planning program," *Studies in Family Planning*, no. 56, pp. 4–18. (Abstract of 1969 report)

Vatuk, Sylvia Jane. 1969. "Kin and neighbors in an urban *mohalla:* a study of white-collar migrants in an Uttar Pradesh city." Unpublished Ph.D. dissertation, Harvard University.

Vig, O. P. 1970. "Demographic effectiveness of sterilization programme in India," *Artha Vijnana* 12:398–405.

Visaria, Pravin. 1971. "Provisional population totals of the 1971 census: some questions and research issues," *Economic and Political Weekly* 6:1459–1466.

Weiner, Myron. 1970. *Perceptions of population change in India: a field report*. Cambridge: Center for International Studies, Massachusetts Institute of Technology.

———. 1971. "Political demography: an inquiry into the political consequences of population change." In *Rapid population growth: consequences and policy implications*. Edited by R. Revelle, pp. 567–617. Baltimore: Johns Hopkins Press.

Wilder, Frank, and D. K. Tyagi. 1968. "India's new departures in mass motivation for fertility control," *Demography* 5:773–779.

Wrigley, E. A. 1969. *Population and history*. New York: World University Library, McGraw-Hill.

Wyon, John B., and John E. Gordon. 1971. *The Khanna study: population problems in the rural Punjab*. Cambridge: Harvard University Press.

Zakaria, Rafiq. 1969. *Family Planning in Maharashtra: a record of bold experiments and significant achievements*. Bombay: Maharashtra State Family Planning Bureau.